THE FUNNIEST COMEDY ICONS OF THE 20TH CENTURY: VOL 2

The Funniest Comedy Icons of the 20th Century, Volume 2 by John Stanley
© 2016, ALL RIGHTS RESERVED
No part of this book may be reproduced in any form or by any means, electronic, mechanical, digital, photocopying, or recording, except for inclusion of a review, without permission in writing from the publisher or John Stanley.

Published in the USA by:
BearManor Media
P O Box 71426
Albany, Georgia 31708
www.bearmanormedia.com

ISBN: 978-1-59393-910-6

BearManor Media, Albany, Georgia
Printed in the United States of America
Book design by Robbie Adkins, www.adkinsconsult.com

THE FUNNIEST COMEDY ICONS OF THE 20TH CENTURY

Volume 2

By John Stanley

To Erica Stanley, my wife for 53 years, who had the pleasure of attending many of the interviews in this book, and who impressed so many comedy stars that they often autographed photos to her instead of me. On the set of Rawhide in 1963, just before I was to interview Clint Eastwood, he suddenly recognized Erica as the receptionist from the Silverado Country Club in Napa, where Clint had often played golf and tennis with his parents in 1958. He shouted out her name and came walking toward her. Me he didn't know from Adam.

To our daughter Trista (left), who lives on the outskirts of Davis, CA, and now has three children: Meghan (next to Trista) at 14 has demonstrated an unusual talent for writing dark poetry and fiction; Lillith (third from left) at 12 is a wonderful dancer and philosopher; and Harper at 5 is already mastering the art of music with his own set of drums.

DEDICATION

A few thank yous to:

RAY K. GOMAN, comedian . . . you were among the funniest of San Francisco comedians in the 1960s, and one of the first stand-up artists I ever interviewed. And you were very terrifying as that PR guy in the horror film, *Nightmare in Blood*.

CLIFF DEKTAR, Hollywood publicist . . . you opened the door to some of Hollywood's biggest stars for two decades long.

AXEL PETERSON, CBS-TV publicist . . . you set me up so I would meet Lucille Ball, Jackie Gleason, and Art Carney in one evening, and they were just three out of hundreds.

DAVID KLEINBERG, my *San Francisco Chronicle* editor for thirteen years and my boss as an Elderhostel instructor for seventeen years. You allowed me to describe to my senior-citizen audiences the comedy stars featured in this book.

EVELYN and BARRY ADLER and JEAN and GARY BLACKBURN, Elderhostel co-ordinators . . . not a single one of you fell asleep during my classes.

You all helped to make this book possible!

TABLE OF CONTENTS

DEDICATION V
INTRODUCTION viii
SHELLEY BERMAN 2
CAROL CHANNING 8
JIM NABORS 17
RONNIE SCHELL 28
RICHARD KIEL (JAWS) 44
CHUCK JONES 49
TOM HANKS 58
CAROL BURNETT 68
JAMES COCO 77
ADRIENNE BARBEAU 85
CONRAD BAIN 94
SALLY STRUTHERS 98
JEAN STAPLETON 104
BARBARA FELDON (*GET SMART*) 108
ED PLATT (*GET SMART*) 114
DON ADAMS (*GET SMART*) 118
PAT PAULSEN 123
THE SMOTHERS BROTHERS 130
MARY TYLER MOORE 136
VICKI LAWRENCE 140
HARVEY KORMAN 145
TIM CONWAY 149
ERNIE ANDERSON 155
GALE GORDON 160
PHYLLIS DILLER 166

KEN CURTIS 174
DOM DELUISE 179
JERRY COLONNA. 185
BARBARA EDEN. 188
GEORGE CARLIN 194
FRANK FONTAINE 198
CLORIS LEACHMAN 202
DICK SHAWN 209
BOB NEWHART 214
OTHER BOOKS BY THE AUTHOR. 222

INTRODUCTION

Welcome to a continuation of what I hope will be a unique excursion into the world of comedy entertainment as told through my exclusive interviews with major celebrities from the worlds of movies, television, and night clubs. Each has his or her own unique twist of humor.

In most cases, these pieces have not been reprinted since they first appeared in the pages of the *San Francisco Chronicle*'s Sunday *Datebook*, otherwise known as "The Pinkie" because of the pink paper on which it was printed. *Datebook* was my home for thirty-three years.

In addition to writing film reviews and book reviews for other departments at the paper, I was granted the pleasure of covering the major personalities who dominated the entertainment world from 1961 through 1993.

Also during that same period, I hosted *Creature Features*, a popular Bay Area Saturday night movie for six years. Two years after leaving the *San Francisco Chronicle*, I became a teacher for Elderhostel (now known as Road Scholar), thanks to the fact that the man who hired me for this new job was also my *Datebook* editor for thirteen years. David Kleinberg, who has gone on to become a stand-up comedian and one-act showman himself, personally tutored me in the art of teaching classes that were all related to show business. They stretched from the history of Jewish comedy to the story of Walt Disney to how Louis Armstrong gave jazz a new meaning to why Frank Sinatra achieved his success in so many different styles. Also sprinkled into the mix were my histories of famous Hollywood women, screen composers Max Steiner and Miklos Rozsa, and the development of Hollywood movie comedies over several decades. It was a never-ending joy that lasted for seventeen years.

In BearManor Media's first edition of *The Funniest Icons of the 20th Century*, I opened with my interviews with Sid Caesar, who in person was anything but funny. In fact, as you're going to find out in this edition, as well as the first, every person had their tragic moments, and sometimes those lasted a lifetime.

In my first interview with Sid, he recounted the horrors of his career, when alcohol and drugs almost brought him to the edge of mental and physical collapse. Our second meeting a few years later revealed how he had fought off his addictions and found the confidence to return to the stage and travel the country with his one-time costar, Imogene Coca, re-creating the comedic characters they had first presented on their TV shows of the early 1950s.

Then, there was my meeting with Bob Hope at his home in Toluca Lake, a suburb of Los Angeles, on the eve of his ninetieth birthday. He so beautifully recounted, sometimes wistfully, sometimes wittily, his fifty years of performances on radio, television, and movies. Especially poignant were his memories of entertaining troops on his USO tours during World War II, Korea, and Vietnam. He broke down sobbing when visiting wounded American soldiers in an Oakland hospital.

In the case of his costar in the Road Pictures, Bing Crosby . . . well, he seemed more serene and cerebral as he sat in the library of his Hillsborough mansion with his hunting companion Remus, a Labrador Retriever, curled up nearby. "I just sing the way it comes out when I open my mouth," was one of Bing's explanations about his career as a singer that I will never forget.

Incredibly funny from the first moment to the last of our meeting at his office in Hollywood was George Burns, who seemed to have a comedic way of answering any question, who could take any fact from his past and give it a one-liner twist. Ah, an evening with Lucille Ball in the backyard of her home on Roxbury Drive in Beverly Hills, with her poodle dog Ginger bouncing up and down at her high heels as she told me how much she hated running Desilu Studios after her divorce from Desi Arnaz, and how she just wanted to be home to raise her children. Also there that night were dour Art Carney and hysterically funny Jackie Gleason. I would meet Gleason again at a theater in San Diego, CA, as he prepared to star in the play *Sly Fox*. (Not much later he suffered a severe heart attack from which he barely survived.)

There were so many others in that first book whom I cannot forget. Audrey Meadows, Gleason's costar on *The Honeymooners* series; Milton Berle (my childhood favorite in the days when television was a burgeoning source of entertainment, and some of the craziest things could be experimented with). The late Joan Rivers still ranks in my mind as one of a kind, especially her remark about her late husband and how she intended to spend each day with him, given that his ashes had been scattered at Neiman-Marcus. Ah, the memories left behind by those satiric souls.

Please do not consider these interviews as mere leftovers; these personalities are beloved, at least by those who remember them and new fans recently discovering them. Among the most memorable was Cloris Leachman, who came on my *Creature Features* show, (which I hosted in the San Francisco-Bay Area for six years), to promote a new *Herbie* movie from Walt Disney.

Because I served as a horror host on the Bay Area's *Creature Features* program, you're even going to visit the Palace of Mystery within Hollywood's Magic Castle and meet a horror host named Ghoulardi (aka Ernie Anderson), along with Elvira (aka Cassandra Peterson), Zacherley (aka John Zacherle) and Joe Bob Briggs (aka John Irving Bloom).

Fans of Old Time Radio will love meeting Gale Gordon, who played Major LaTrivia on *The Fibber McGee and Molly Show*. There's also Jerry Colonna, who was Bob Hope's second banana during his radio days.

I would like to give a special nod to Adrienne Barbeau, whose career has stretched from playing the divorced daughter on *Maude* to horror roles in films she appeared in with her former husband, John Carpenter. She sent me some updated material just for this edition.

There was nothing to laugh at during my interview with comedian-actor James Coco, who was promoting a cookbook that was also about his personal problems caused by overeating and popping plenty of pills. He almost went totally berserk as we were finishing our lunch, screaming across the dining room that I was a fake journalist. It all had to do with his illnesses, not mine.

If you loved reading about Mel Blanc in the first edition, telling us how he created the voices for Bugs Bunny and other popular Warner Bros. cartoon greats, you don't want to miss this edition's interview with Chuck Jones, who helped in the creation of Bugs Bunny and Wile E. Coyote, and scores of other cartoon characters. During one of our interviews, he drew some original cartoon art for me, which is in print for the first time in this volume.

Western fans will discover Ken Curtis, who played Festus, that hillbilly deputy who walked the streets of Dodge City for many years on TV's *Gunsmoke*. Ken will tell you where he picked up that memorable drawl of his.

Get Smart fans, get wiser. You're going to meet Maxwell Smart (Don Adams), as well as Agent 99 (Barbara Feldon) and Chief (Ed Platt).

How fortunate to have spent a couple of hours with Moe Howard, boss man of The Three Stooges, at Columbia Studios in Hollywood, when he was just entering the twilight years of his career. Find out what it was like to head up one of the goofiest teams of slapstick comedy.

How fortunate to be the first person from a newspaper ever to interview Jim Nabors, who would go on to costar in the Andy Griffith TV series before getting his own series, *Gomer Pyle–USMC*. Through Nabors I met his costar and close friend Ronnie Schell, who also proved to be a long-lasting comedian and expert at doing voices for TV commercials. Ronnie and I would come together at rare moments as if we were old pals. Ronnie is still busily performing in night clubs and aboard cruise ships, and he sent some new material to use in this book.

What an intriguing world the world of entertainment can be.—
–John Stanley, January 2016, Pacifica, CA 94044

SHELLEY BERMAN
How a Ringing Telephone Almost Destroyed the Career Of Monologue Master Berman

In the beginning, Shelley Berman wanted to be an actor performing on Broadway. However, he wasn't making it as an actor and he desperately needed money, so he designed a stand-up comedy routine. It was only going to tide him over until he could get that Broadway role and prove to the world he was a great actor.

That part of his dream wasn't going to happen.

What did happen was that he proved to the world he was a marvelous monologist. Sitting upright on a tall stool or just standing up on his own two legs, he held a telephone and engaged in a conversation with a son, daughter, or a wife. Fame and success in the world of comedy were miraculously his. He became part of a neo-comedian pack that included Lenny Bruce, Mort Sahl, Mike Nichols, Elaine May, and Dick Gregory. Not just comedians, but social commentators on modern man. A whole new kind of success with comedy began for him.

"No siren ever tempted an Olympian greater than the riches that befell this ordinary man who wanted to be an actor but became a comedian instead." Berman brings a glass of Dewar's on the rocks to his lips, barely taking a sip as he sits at a table in Bardelli's Restaurant, on the edge of San Francisco's Tenderloin. It is September 1981, but Berman, at the age of fifty-six, is no longer the grand comedy star he once was, and he's now ready to admit all his mistakes.

"My albums became the first non-musical Gold Records in recording history, and I appeared in places where comics had never appeared before. But my strength turned into my weakness. I was falling for all that crap about buying ten suits at a time, or walking into an auto showroom and buying a new car without even asking about the price. A wise man would have seen through such crap.

Shelley Berman the way he often looked early in his career, atop a tall stool, engaged in a conversation with family members.

I misled myself so easily. Dumb acceptance of the material things we all think are so wonderful, but which are not fulfilling."

He pushes the glass of Dewar's away. "The Shelley Berman you see on a stool, delivering a comedy routine, as bitingly witty and incisive as he is, represents approximately ten per cent of the man. I allow everyone to see everything about me. I let them see my height, my width, my depth. I'm a man of good words. I'm a man of bad words. I'm a man of kindness and cruelty. I have arrogance and humility. I have a real basic flaw. It's called humanity."

What led to this unusually frank and self-examining human's downfall? In his own words, "Audiences and show producers experienced a negative side to my personality that has been amplified out of all proportion." In short, he adds, "I've developed a reputation for being a pain you-know-where. Words like antagonist, arrogant, rude, and insolent have been used to describe me by my worst critics."

This reputation has lived on with him into a new era, where clearly he wishes it did not follow. He would prefer to be thought of in a mellower, nostalgic light, and that old negative image hanging over his head—which he feels is unjust—does lead to misunderstandings. "You cannot escape being a sonofabitch, once the world has decided you are exactly that."

This image that Shelley Berman was "a sonofabitch" began largely in 1963 after he appeared on a taped episode of *The Du Pont Show of the Week*. He was doing one of his monologues ("a delicate piece of business about a father talking to his son on the phone") when a backstage telephone rang loudly enough to be heard by the audience—and Berman. "What nobody knows is this: I had been interrupted by the same ringing telephone during an earlier taping. I had politely asked that the phone not be allowed to ring again. But, when it rang that second time, I exploded. I really let them have it. But later, in the editing, the producer chose to invert the sequence of events so my angry outburst was shown, without the motivation behind it ever explained." (Berman had been made aware of the re-editing yet still allowed the program to be aired, apparently not realizing the ultimate effect.)

Big mistake, indeed. The viewing world exploded in anger at seeing Berman's outrageous reaction, and the world of comedy production decided maybe Berman wasn't so funny after all. "Working as a comedian became impossible," recalls the comedian, who was repeatedly turned down or just plain ignored afterward. "I turned off the funny business and went somewhere else. I did what I could to ply my trade, though in relative peace."

For almost a decade, he has wandered about America, appearing in various stage productions. That is what has brought him to the Bay Area, to portray Horace Vandergelder in a production of *Hello, Dolly!*

If Berman has a self-image of himself, it is of being "a man and an actor and a comedian. I know I'm good at being those three things. I stubbornly refuse to conform to any image that others have of me. I'm who I am and you can say what you want."

As one in a confessional booth, Berman now tells me that, in the beginning, "I didn't love the people in my audiences so much; they had a less flattering status in my eyes. I think I know what triggered my more affectionate feeling for audiences. It was my son Joshua, who had to die before my values came into new focus. That was a terrible time for me. I was in Cincinnati and I brought him to Children's Hospital so I could be close to him and keep living and do what I had to do. Only twelve, Joshua was dying of cancer. A half hour before the show, *Don't Drink the Water*, everything in my life, other than the theater, stopped. I didn't worry about my wife, my dying son, myself. All I knew was, I wanted to work. I had to work." Joshua died on Oct. 29, 1977, twelve years of age.

Something very strange happens next. Berman toasts me with his half-filled glass of Dewar's, as if he wants to salute me, and then seems to slip off into a kind of reverie, and for the next few minutes talks uninterrupted, almost as though he is delivering a monologue. I just lean back, keep my mouth shut, and scribble notes as fast as I can:

"Comedians are always there when you need them. When the world was in flames, and Germany was destroying Europe and threatening the rest of the world, there was someone who relieved our tensions. He was Danny Kaye with an extraordinary gift

Shelley Berman in the late 1980s.

for nonsense. He'd been there waiting in the wings, and he was there when we needed him.

"Then, when we were trying to survive the peace and there was a growing middle class in America, Sid Caesar, who had been in the wings waiting, was there when we needed him. Just as Jackie Gleason was there when we needed him. And our time and place absorbed them. And then when Joseph McCarthy almost destroyed the dream of America, and we realized we could still talk and say what we wanted in the aftermath, there were comedians who had been waiting who were there when we needed them. Mort Sahl and Lenny Bruce and Shelley Berman and Jonathan Winters.

"And then when Blacks finally franchised and there was violence in the world with napalm and the killing of our young men and our nation rebelled, there were comedians who were there when we needed them. Godfrey Cambridge, Dick Gregory, Don Rickles, Buddy Hackett, and Shecky Greene—articulate spokesmen for American thoughts, and they had been there, waiting to serve us.

"And then when sense became nonsense again and there were oil and gas shortages and energy crises, there were comedians there when we needed them. Steve Martin and Robin Williams. You see, I come from a family of beautiful men and women. We are the articulators of our time. We don't become obsolete. Mister, when you need us, just knock on the door, and we will be there."

Berman drains his Dewar's and puts the glass back on the table. It is clear from his expression that he has nothing further to say. It is like a curtain descends and the act is finished.

Berman has never completely regained his stature as comedian, relying instead on his acting abilities. His roles in movies and TV series, although they have continued, are relatively small. He can be seen as a judge in the feature *Meet the Fokkers* (2004) and he also played Judge Sanders in eleven episodes of *Boston Legal*, all bit roles. He fared a little better playing Larry David's father in seven seasons of *Curb Your Enthusiasm*. In 2012, he accused Bob Newhart of stealing his technique of doing a one-sided telephone conversation. Newhart pointed out that several comedians before Shelley Berman came on the scene had done a similar telephone routine, such as Myron Cohen and Georgie Jessel (who was always calling up his mother).

CAROL CHANNING
Hello, Carol! George Can Be a Girl's Best Friend, Enough To Make You Zany and Whacky as Ever

Wide-eyed, whacky, and with an overconfident stride that suggests she might fall flat on her face at any second, Carol Channing emerges on the stage of the South Shore Room at Harrah's Club, Lake Tahoe, with the same vibrant talent and fresh satire that have been her trademarks for nearly fifteen years.

Carol Channing and George Burns in the summer of 1962, when they briefly worked as a duo.

In summer 1962, Carol and cigar-puffing George Burns have teamed up and gone on the road. Before Lake Tahoe, they had stopped in Seattle at the World's Fair so that George could light his cigar with a Space Needle Lighter and pose for photos before they did their show at the Orpheum Theater. Now, watching these two perform as a team, one can see that it was a good idea. Carol's pantomiming and "dumb blonde" routines, which began on Broadway stages, are still her chief show business attributes, and George . . . well, George will always be George, slowing puffing on a new cigar and providing the lines that Carol needs to sparkle like a diamond, which in this case is George's Best Friend.

Carol, she's screwball through and through. Her voice is grotesquely exaggerated—loud, squawking, and almost hoarse. Her trim figure and blonde hair give her a seductive look and supply an added oomph to her comedy when she presents her impersonation of Marlene Dietrich. Scantily clad as the German actress, she mutters, "If my grandmother had worn this costume, she would have inherited my grandfather's pension six years earlier." In her as-Brigitte-Bardot-would-portray-Lady Macbeth sketch, she switches the famous sleepwalking scene to the bathtub. Towel-covered a la Bardot, she mutters: "You may join me in the bath, Mac, but don't make a wave." It's all done in elegant, fumbling fashion, accented by exact caricature and duplication of voices. George stands there and twinkles.

The dialogues between Carol and Burns? They are reminiscent of the days when Burns and Allen (Gracie retired since 1958 because of angina, a moment that was reported in *Life* magazine with her photo on the cover) were a popular couple on radio and TV shows. The inanity of Carol's speech and her clumsy gesturing give them a refreshing newness.

That newness can only add to the range of talent Carol has shown since 1949, when on Broadway she began portraying Lorelei Lee in *Gentlemen Prefer Blondes*. To Carol's disappointment, that role went to Marilyn Monroe when Fox produced the feature-film version in 1953, with Jane Russell costarring.

In her dressing room at Harrah's, as she relaxes in fluffy red slippers and tights, Carol is still bubbling with the same vitality she has amply demonstrated during the show, and she repeatedly expresses delight with her new partnership.

"Me and George," she tells me, "we've been the best of friends for more than seven years. And one night last year, George asked me to do The Twist with him at a party we were attending. A couple of important Hollywood agents happened to be there that night, and when they saw the two of us on the dance floor, they felt it was real chemistry. So did I.

"One of the agents said to me: 'You two oughta team up.' George and I looked at each other, laughing at the idea. But nobody said anything further and we all went home. Then in London, not long after, while we were staying at the Dorchester Hotel, we did a soft-shoe number in front of the one and only Jack Benny. Jack thought we were great. Given that and The Twist, our act was born."

The first place they performed at was the Dunes Hotel in Las Vegas, followed by their Seattle appearances. Carol goes on. "We were going to New York next to film a TV spectacular, but unfortunately we have to break up the team for a while because I have to go into rehearsal for my next play, *King's Mare*. It's a comedy, but it's my first straight role. I play Anne of Cleves, the only wife of Henry VIII who wasn't beheaded. During the entire first act, I speak only German, so the part calls for pantomime to convey much of the meaning. I'm hoping that heads will roll—with laughter."

King's Mare is by Anita Loos, who also wrote *Gentlemen Prefer Blondes*, in which Carol became famous for playing the diamond-clad, sexually exciting Lorelei Lee. Carol has already been promised the part of Anne in the screen version. (Her only other film until now was a turgid 1956 entry entitled *The First Traveling Saleslady*, and she grimaces at the mere mention of the title.)

After the pair leaves Tahoe, it may be a long while before they return under the same billing. That depends on the outcome of *King's Mare*. You can rely on Carol to entertain you in one form or another. "I can't do anything else," she admits candidly. "Show business, and the art of comedy, that's all I know."

Carol and George did not perform together again, nor did *King's Mare* make it to the stage, but she went on to portray Dolly Levi in *Hello, Dolly!* on Broadway two years later, winning a Tony

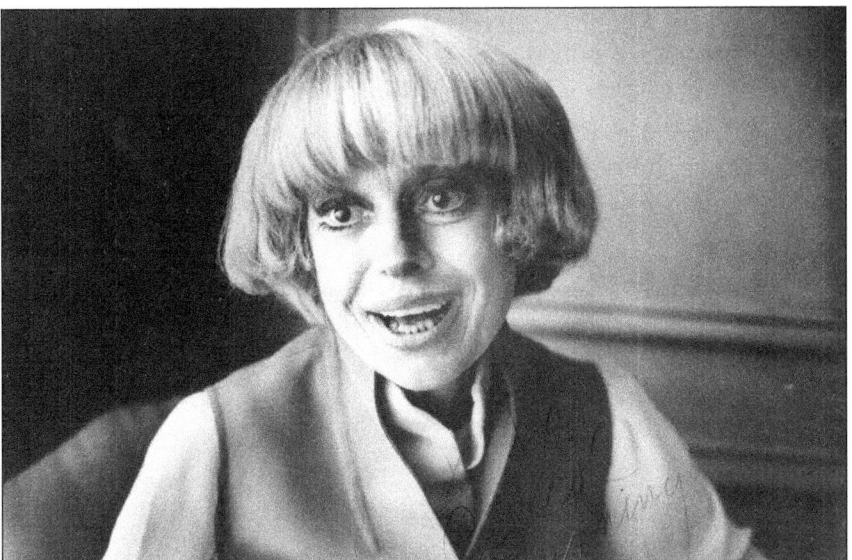

Carol Channing signed this publicity photo during our luncheon interview in 1983, to which she brought her charm, sense of humor, and her own canisters filled with food to satisfy her personal tastes. She signed with a red pen but it's barely discernible.

Award. She kept herself in the spotlight with *Thoroughly Modern Millie* (1967) with her portrayal of Muzzy Van Hossmere, for which she was nominated for an Oscar.

Now, we come to July 1983, when she would star in a road production of *Hello, Dolly!* at San Francisco's Orpheum Theater. The *San Francisco Chronicle* assigned me to cover the event in advance, and we met a few days prior to the opening night performance.

Carol is back in town. She refuses to let go of her *Dolly*, and baby, you can almost feel the room swayin'. She's just swept into the posh dining room at the Clift Hotel, a place that holds fond memories, because she used to pass in front of the Clift every Sunday morning on her way to a nearby Christian Science church, when she was growing up in San Francisco.

At the age of sixty-two, sparkling like a diamond is still her keynote. Heads are turning at the brightness of her red pants suit. Heads are turning for the megastar. Her 5' 9" frame passes the staring faces with confident strides and slides smoothly into a chair at a corner table that has been reserved for just the two of us.

She has just flown in from Portland, Oregon and looks radiant and triumphant, carrying her success in her eyes. Her lips are pursed curiously, as if a question is always bubbling to be asked. Her hair is a platinum color, cropped close and presumably a wig. (At least she has admitted to wearing a wig in public since her once "golden" hair became an unsightly ashy color after years of bleaching.)

Strains of *Hello, Dolly!* drift from the adjoining bar-lounge, courtesy of a pianist who knows what to play when a star is supping in the next room. It is fanfare not only to her presence but to *Hello, Dolly!* itself, which Carol is about to bring from Portland to San Francisco for a three-week run.

Not just any old *Hello, Dolly!* but a recreated slice of theatrical history, a revival of the original Tony-winning musical-comedy production as it was first presented on Broadway at the St. James Theater for 2,884 performances under the direction of Gower Champion. Same choreography, same dance numbers, same sets, all reconstructed from the original blueprints, music sheets, dancing charts, wardrobe designs, and memories of those who participated during those golden moments in the 1960s.

Dinner with Carol Channing is no ordinary event. Because she doesn't like to be surrounded by irrelevant distractions, she insists that only she and I be seated at the table. The rest of her entourage—husband Charles Lowe, Orpheum publicist, etc.—must remain at bay at a nearby table.

Even the process of eating seems a step removed from normal as Carol, seated in the very heart of this gourmet dining room, opens her carry-all purse and plunks down a number of silver canisters, thermos and flasks, each engraved with her name. She doesn't even look at the menu—anything from the kitchen, she says, could contain "chemicals and impurities" and instantly set off one of the allergies that have plagued her for many years. Those allergies extend to chlorine poisoning, which means even a glass of water is taboo.

So, wincing a little because she's a lover of good foods, she picks up one of the canisters and dumps out her main course: Finely diced raw carrots. Her chaser is a glass of distilled water.

Carol Channing portraying Dolly Levy, the role she created on Broadway in Hello, Dolly!

Other canisters contain celery sticks, cucumber slices, and sesame seeds—organically grown foods from special soil, flown from Southern California to wherever she is in the world at any given engagement.

As she looks in her photographs, Carol always appears larger than life, not unlike a certain matchmaker, named Dolly Gallagher Levi, whom she has been known to play on occasion. Perhaps you could call this tightly controlling your image before the public. Even conversation with her takes on a strange twist. Questions about glamour, love, sex appeal, fame, fortune, and beauty and what it's like to be at the top-of-the-theater-pack all receive the same kind of gasping of breath, helpless shrugging of the shoulders and an enlarging of her playful eyes, as if you've just asked her to explain in twenty-five words or less the meaning of life.

Glamour? Little old her? Fame? Why, she's just a kid who used to live at 1230 Washington Street and who went to Lowell High and who received a free trip to Hawaii once because she won a classroom oral contest entitled "What Does America Mean to Me?"

Always that control of image, as her answers are directed away from Carol Channing The Individual, as though that is either too private to get involved with, or she really isn't worth the time and effort to discuss. Directed away from Private/Self-Effacing Carol Channing, her answer is rerouted to Channing The Actress, heavily engaged in playing the role of Dolly. She says at one point: "I'm selling Dolly, not myself. If I was selling only myself I would be egotistical. I would lack perception and insight. What do I care what I'm like? I'm not playing me. I have no knack for selling myself. If I did, I'd be pretty bloody boring."

If she was like Dolly, she adds, "I wouldn't be funny on the stage. Audiences know that I'm nothing like Dolly Levy; they know she's a satire of a yenta [Yiddish for "matchmaker" or "busybody"] of the first order. She's a woman with push and shove, who wheels everyone around. She'll stop at no subterfuge to get her man. She can be awful and irritating. And all that has *nothing* to do with me."

She says the same thing is true of that legendary flapper, Lorelei Lee, of Anita Loos' comedy, *Gentlemen Prefer Blondes*, which Carol created and immortalized on Broadway in 1949 with the help of the song "Diamonds Are a Girl's Best Friend."

"Loos insisted on me for the part," recalls Carol, "because I wasn't the cutest girl they auditioned. Anita wanted me because she saw that I could give her play the satirical edge it needed." The personal need for diamonds never transferred to Carol, however. "Do I wear diamonds? No, they're not becoming on me. I'm six-foot in heels and the only rock that's flattering on me is the Hope Diamond."

Nor has her elaborate stage wardrobes rubbed off on her private life. "I'm very conservative when it comes to clothing," she explains. "I have one good outfit for each occasion. I travel so much I don't have time to fool around with big wardrobes. It's too much to pack and unpack."

Don't ask Carol about the negative side to her life—her weaknesses as an actress or the hardships of being a recognizable personality in public. She'll only look puzzled again and shift into positive gear and call herself fortunate. "I'm very fortunate," she elaborates, "to be playing a character I'm crazy about. I never grow tired of Dolly because every night on the stage is a challenge to me to make it seem like I'm playing Dolly for the very first time. I have that responsibility to the audience. Otherwise, I have no right to enter the theater."

She pauses. "Excuse me, but I'm a food voyeur. May I look at your food?" She leans closer to my plate, staring into a goblet of jumbo prawns, her eyes flaming with a new kind of hunger. "Those are the wonderful, juicy kind," she observes. "I used to get them at Fisherman's Wharf. Popped them into my mouth like pieces of popcorn. You should go there to get them . . . what am I saying. You probably can't get them at the Wharf anymore . . . you aren't going to put them into that red goop, are you? That'll spoil their sweetness."

The "red goop" is taken away untouched and the waiter replaces it with a Chef's Salad. "You've selected the right dressing," says Carol, living up to her words of being a voyeur, pressing keenly toward my plate for a closer look at strips of yellow cheese and chopped-up turkey and ham. She comments on the texture of the lettuce. "Are the radishes good?" she asks, helpless not to ask. Texture . . . radishes . . . I just keep on chewing.

She straightens up and picks at her raw carrots. "Our producer, James Nederlander, gave me the choice of one city to play in before we leave for a European tour and I picked San Francisco. It's the only choice. This city will always be my home. Growing up, I used to sit in the balcony of the Orpheum and awe over the stars. It was the ultimate escape for me. It takes your life out of the factual and the mundane, the theater. It sets me soaring."

After San Francisco, the troupe will be soaring off to Copenhagen, Munich, Monte Carlo, Paris, Rome. For each country she has memorized phonetically an opening curtain speech. Traveling with her, as he always does, will be her husband Charles, the one-time producer of the George Burns-Gracie Allen radio and TV shows. He now devotes his life as much to Dolly as Carol.

In November, after the tour, Carol will begin rehearsals for a new play by Jerry Herman, who co-wrote *Hello, Dolly!* with Michael Stewart. It's called *The Follies* and, according to Carol, "not even God knows where the laughs are yet. All you can do is cross your fingers and work hard and hope for a success. About ninety per cent of new shows are smash flops."

For a while, Carol talks about the worldwide popularity of *Hello, Dolly:* how Dolly was originally a character in Thornton Wilder's

The Matchmaker; how the play has been translated into almost every language in the world; how there have been so many different versions, some of them highly stylized; and how the current production is "religiously faithful" to the original.

Then, they signal from the other table that Carol must leave immediately to catch a plane back to Portland, for she has a show this very night. She's already stayed a little too long; the chauffeur will have to rush her to the airport. She gathers up her canisters, flasks, and thermos and stuffs them into her oversized purse, and she takes the time to pause and comment, one final time, on her dedication. "I'm dedicated to the character of Dolly. She's brought me enormous success. And I want to give it right back to her."

Lowe continued to manage Carol's career until 1998, when she suddenly accused him of mental and physical abuse and filed for divorce. He died before it was final. Her autobiography, *Just Lucky, I Guess: A Memoir of Sorts*, was published in 2003. She has since lost another husband and survived a bout with ovarian cancer. She lives on and so does Dolly, in the hearts and minds of those who saw her performing as one of the most unforgettable characters in the history of Broadway musicals.

JIM NABORS
In the Beginning, the Hillbilly Opera Singer of . . . Sylacauga? Shazam! One Oddball Baritone

Jim Nabors was a comedy entertainer I would cross paths with several times, beginning in the fall of 1962 when he made his initial appearance at San Francisco's Purple Onion, one of the most popular comedy clubs during the so-called Hip Era. He would go on to become a major TV star, and we continued to meet off and on over the years. He would tell me after the first story appeared in print that I was the very first person to write him up in a major newspaper. Therefore, he was always glad to see me and treated me warmly. Here's how it all started.

The lights in the Purple Onion have dimmed. The introductory applause is over, and now everyone is waiting for comedian Jim Nabors—a performer nobody in the area has seen perform in this club before—to begin his act. The question that pops to mind when Nabors opens his mouth is whether he is really a comedian, for when Nabors finally makes a noise, no great pearls of wit fill the air—just a magnificent baritone voice singing a classical piece of opera.

Suddenly, the baritone is lost when the tempo of the music changes. Now bounding energetically through the smoky air is a ridiculous hillbilly squalling, as if it had floated in all the way from the Ozarks. The contrast and abrupt switch from the deep baritone to the Deep South has the crowd in stitches—and no sooner has this begun than it is time once again for the solemn Nabors, as if he were part of the Brooklyn Tabernacle Choir.

Well, that's Jim Nabors for you, unpredictable and ingeniously original. He gradually works into the thick of his act, combining the baritone with humorous lyrics and relying on his Southern accent to carry him between songs as he converses delightfully with members of the audience.

Jim Nabors signed this photo to me and Erica sometime early in his career, when he was still climbing up the ranks to reach Private Pyle. It reads, "To John and Erika: My best to you always. It's a pleasure to call you my friend."

Once the laughter has died away and Nabors is not centered in the spotlight, he appears to be as homespun as some of his songs and mannerisms presented on stage. Although enthusiastic over what he considers his first big nightclub engagement in San Francisco (and almost anywhere else in America), he remains a down-to-earth young man, who hopes to continue his career and some day make a greater name for himself on Broadway.

Nabors is really new to show business, at least on the West Coast. A native-born Alabaman, he was reared in a place called Sylacauga ("that means," he will soon tell me backstage, "Buzzard Roost in Creek Indian"), and is a graduate of the University of Alabama. He had his own TV show in Chattanooga and was a recording artist for Roulette Records.

Less than a year ago, however, he was in Hollywood working for NBC-TV as a film editor and singing part-time at a night spot in Santa Monica called The Horn.

"I was doing the singing just for kicks," says Nabors, resting in his dressing room after the show, "until one night Carol Burnett, who was connected with Steve Allen at the time, saw my routine and was impressed enough to mention me to her associates. Six months later, I was written into one of her TV skits. It went over good, and consequently I appeared in sixty shows with Steve Martin."

What is perhaps most unusual about Nabors is his complete lack of prior singing instruction. "What I do out on that stage is only a satirical approach to music," he explains. "I use my operatic voice primarily for laughs. So I've never had a singing teacher or a music lesson in my life. And occasionally I startle the pants off someone when they ask me who my teacher was and I have to tell them there never was a teacher. A lot of them go away shaking their heads, finding it hard to believe. I guess I am a little hard to believe. Sometimes I wonder about myself, myself."

It wasn't very long until I met Jim Nabors again. This time it was April 1964, and I was now covering stories in the heart of Hollywood.

The U.S. Marine Corps in 1964 has had it. If you thought *semper fidelis* leathernecks were having a rough time soldiering on *The Lieutenant,* an NBC training program that is about as tasty as a K-ration, wait until next fall when a recruit named Gomer Pyle will be standing tall, stiff at attention, on the CBS lineup. Call it a private affair! Gomer, the gas man from *The Andy Griffith Show* will soon be Private Pyle. Gaaawwwleee!

There is a saving grace that may keep *Gomer Pyle - USMC* from turning into a viewing booby trap. Military life will be maintained

Another signed photo from Jim Nabors, this time during his success on Gomer Pyle - USMC. This one was directed to my wife Erica. It reads: "Lovely lady and good friend. Gomer says hey."

strictly by NOP (Nonstandard Operational Procedures). Marion Hargrove and the Sad Sack will have nothing on Private Pyle when his weekly misadventures in boot camp with a growling sergeant (Frank Sutton) are televised this fall on Friday nights.

Portraying the innocuous dunce will be Jim Nabors, an amiable young actor, who was fortunate enough to land his own series after three years of Prime Time exposure to the public on *The Andy Griffith Show* (1962-1964). I first met Nabors in 1962, the night he premiered at the Purple Onion nightclub in San Francisco. I like to think that because he told me soon after that I was the very first journalist ever to interview him, that perhaps I gave him a shove in the right direction. The gangling, Alabama-born performer almost immediately was cast as a gas station attendant named Gomer Pyle on *The Andy Griffith Show*, and appeared in his first episode in December 1962. Gomer was to appear in many more episodes and also has had one-time shots in the series *Mr. Smith Goes to Washington* and *The Great Adventure*.

Naiveté, as you might have suspected, is the key to our hero's misfortunes. "I like Gomer a whole lot," Jim tells me during one of my trips to Hollywood. "He's an easy character to play but he still has lots of qualities—some of them I wish I had. And I try to convey a rural personality a la the Ozarks." He achieves this with his drawling voice and rustic simplicity. "He's real likable, very trustworthy, and would never dream of anybody doing him wrong, or visa versa."

How did his role on *The Andy Griffith Show* happen? "It was just after the Purple Onion. I returned to The Horn in Santa Monica, where one night Andy caught my act and decided the singing might fit for an upcoming role on his show. He felt Gomer clicked well for the kind of people who lived in Mayberry, and I was signed on as a permanent member of the cast."

In the final show of the 1964 season, Gomer leaves Mayberry to join the Marines, so the sequence of events now allows him to turn up soon in his own show. This kind of episode is called a spin-off, in which Griffith takes a back seat so the script can focus on a character headed into his own series.

It was on the basis of this one comedy, written and directed by Aaron Rubin, that *Gomer Pyle - USMC* was purchased and a deal made for thirty-four episodes. Come summer, Nabors will don green fatigues and combat boots to go before the cameras, with interiors being shot in one of the Desilu sound stages and exteriors done at the Culver City lot known as Forty Acres.

Frank Sutton as Gunnery Sergeant Vince Carter and Jim Nabors as Gomer Pyle in CBS' hit sitcom Gomer Pyle - USMC.

There is nothing phony in Nabors' approach to human relationships, he tells me. He sincerely likes people and has such a friendly nature that he couldn't be any other way, no matter how hard he tried. Because success has come so swiftly to this gentle young man, leaving him a bit starry-eyed and agape over the prospects of a glamorous Hollywood career, it is almost as though Gomer Pyle and not Jim Nabors has become a TV star.

I would have another meeting with Jim Nabors in April 1965, when he stopped over in San Francisco to have lunch with me at the Red Knight Restaurant. It was a "private" meeting, more like a meeting between two friends rather than a newsman interviewing a celebrity. Nabors was still the same "aww shucks" kind of guy, still shy, affable, and still the yokel.

Once there was a Hollywood film cutter who hung up his scissors and paste pot to take his first professional booking as a singer-comedian in North Beach's Purple Onion nightclub.

He possessed a magnificent baritone, with which he delivered flawless operatic selections, and he was capable of offsetting the solemnity of his act with some hillbilly squalling.

Offstage, he was shy, unsure of his footing, inexperienced in the ways of the nightclub world. He was bewildered, being centered so suddenly in the spotlight, and he often voiced his dismay to friends.

Today, three years and thousands of feet of celluloid later, Nabors is still that shy young man with an unpretentious, affable nature, almost as though he hasn't yet realized he has become a national pastime, and a beloved personality who will be remembered by his generation.

As star of *Gomer Pyle - USMC*, the week-to-week misadventures of a hayseed in the barracks who expresses himself with "Hey" and "Shazam," Nabors has achieved the overnight success story.

The unchanged Nabors joins me for lunch and opens up with "I'm not one of those actors who gets frustrated, or allows his ego to get the best of him, or thinks he's typecast just because he's been playing the same role for more than a month."

Nabors, soon to have a new record album in release which features such songs as "You Can't Go Roller Skating in a Buffalo Stampede," will soon be demonstrating his vocal/comedy talents in the South Shore Room at Harrah's Tahoe.

It will be his second appearance at Harrah's Tahoe. "Me and Andy, that's Andy Griffith, played there last April." With Nabors this time will be Frank Sutton (the hard-boiled Sergeant Carter.)

I am destined to meet Jim Nabors one final time, in June 1972, at his home in Bel Air, an affluent neighborhood of West Side Los Angeles, where the singing hillbilly is still riding high.

Although his Gomer Pyle image is only ten years old, it is an image that seems as far away as a nebula and as unreal as a dream, as though it happened several lifetimes ago. Or maybe it never happened at all!

Perhaps this strange feeling of distance and unreality is caused by the way success makes once ordinary people seem like something greater, and totally different, from their former selves.

That image enacted originally within the Purple Onion nightclub. Jim Nabors, a nobody from nowhere, gangling and awkward, "aw shucks" in a genuine sort of way, steps onto the stage in a checkered shirt, Levi's, and squashed hat and begins singing like a hillbilly. Squalling might be a more apt term than singing, but whichever you choose, the audience sat in a stupefied state, not knowing whether to clear their throats politely or applaud out of pure sympathy.

But no sooner had Nabors established this high-pitched tomfoolery when he switched to a deep baritone voice that took on all the polish and sophistication of a Metropolitan opera singer. The contrast was a winner. While an Onion audience, considered very "in" in those days (and nights), would never have settled for a hillbilly or opera singer singly, the two together—in this strange embodiment known as Jim Nabors—proved to be the North Beach hit of 1962.

That's the image as we remember it, and that's the image that Nabors took with him to Los Angeles, where he was soon discovered by Andy Griffith, and signed to play Gomer Pyle. Not even Griffith had foreseen what was to happen: Nabors started to sing in the series besides just pumping gas, and he started getting bigger moments on camera. Next thing you know, the writers were spinning Nabors off to join the Marines in *Gomer Pyle - USMC*.

Nabors became one of the big stars in the CBS line-up, voluntarily giving up Gomer after six seasons in favor of an hour-long variety series, *The Jim Nabors Hour*.

For almost seven years, Nabors was riding high on success, with never a cancellation, never a setback, and always plenty of work: guest appearances, tours, new record albums. It was non-stop, and he thrived on every waking moment of it.

Jim Nabors as he appeared on his one-hour variety series in 1970.

In early 1971, he was faced with his first major disappointment. His variety series, although tops in the ratings jungle, was cancelled. It was a cold, calculated move by CBS, which was ruthlessly cleaning out anything that had a rural taint to it. Hillbillies, no matter what kind of voice they delivered in, and even if they came from Beverly, were strictly for the pastures. Times, they were a-changin', and Nabors had been deeply affected.

Recently, Nabors poured himself a soft drink in the front room of his lavish home in Bel Air and ruminated about that moment in his career. 'Yeah, I guess you could say I was a little upset about the variety show being pulled out from under me. I didn't think we deserved to be cancelled. Our ratings were very good, but we sort of got lumped with all those other country shows. Maybe you could call me country a little bit, but certainly not the rest of the cast."

Nabors, never one to sit around and mope or remain idle beyond a twenty-minute pause, immediately began making new plans. "I got on the phone the very same day," he recalls, sipping his soda, "and started mapping out a summer-long tour that took me to Lake Tahoe, Baltimore, Washington, Dallas, Kansas City, St. Louis, Detroit, Chicago. It wasn't a question of dollars and cents, or image, or even pride. I just wanted to work, to stay busy, to get back on the stage where I could do the only thing I really know—entertain."

It proved to be good therapy because by the time he returned to Los Angeles he had three records albums waiting to be cut, and had been signed for TV shows coming up this fall, including a TV special of his own.

Now he is busy preparing another summer-long tour that will bring him to the Circle Star Theater in San Carlos, just south of San Francisco. From there, he will play across the country.

"I'd like very much to get back into TV with another series," Jim tells me, somewhat hopefully. "Exactly what kind of series . . . I'm not going to be insistent about that. Perhaps even a movie. I've never made a movie, and it always seems like people have to see you in one before you get any offers. But I'm still waiting for someone to offer me the right role."

Meanwhile, Gomer Pyle, whether a gas pumper or a "Shazam" Marine, lives on in Nabors' heart in the form of syndication residuals, as the series plays stations nationwide to fill the afternoon gaps. "I have a piece of Gomer," he says with a grin. "That's the only way to play a hillbilly."

Jim Nabors did continue working in television but it was on a limited basis and he would not have another weekly show of his own until 1978, a daytime affair called, oddly enough, *The Jim Nabors Show*. It brought him an Emmy nomination but the series was short-lived. As for making movies, he would become friends with Burt Reynolds and have supporting roles in *The Best Little Whorehouse in Texas* (1982), *Stroker Ace* (1983) and *Cannonball II* (1984). Nabors ended up moving to the Hawaiian island of Maui, where he now owns 20,000 macadamia trees. In 2013, at the age of eighty-two, he married his long-time living partner, Stan Cadwallader. (There had been rumors back in the 1980s that he and Rock Hudson were lovers, a controversial moment for them both, for although they had been friends, they reportedly never saw each other afterward.)

RONNIE SCHELL
Who Shoots for the Hip, Became The Slowest Fastest Rising Young Comedian

Ronnie Schell will start out as a stand-up comedian who was a part of the so-called Hip Generation, a handful of comedians who twisted humor in the direction of social issues. Think of Lenny Bruce and Shelley Berman as his counterparts. Then, to my utter surprise, Schell became one of Jim Nabors' co-stars on *Gomer Pyle - USMC*. I will run into him several times in the years to come, but we first meet in early 1969.

Onto the stage of Bimbo's 365 Club bounces Ronnie, all put-on smile and fast chatter. He paces tensely, gripping his microphone as though it were a live hand grenade, telling the audience to cool it when the applause reaches an exuberance even he can't accept.

Did everyone know there is a controversial article about him? Yes, it ran yesterday in the November *Watchtower*. As for Black Power, it is merely prune juice.

Ronnie does a vignette. Vignettes, he notes, have kept him out of the big time for many years. He sits on a stool ("my potty complex," he explains). There follows a series of sketches about a drunken bus driver, a little old lady, and a gay movie extra.

This is the comedy of Ronnie Schell, who was born in nearby Richmond, CA, attended San Francisco State and grew up in the very heart of San Francisco's entertainment world, working his way to the top of stand-up comedy even before he graduated from SF State. He was once considered a hip comic. He roved in the same lucrative pastures of social satire as Lenny Bruce, Mort Sahl, and Shelley Berman. Maybe he never quite reached their pinnacles of satire but he was always there, struggling on the edges, and "mingling," as he likes to put it.

How the mighty have fallen. No, no. Ronnie intentionally shirked the hip comic image a long time ago because he saw it dying, saw the hip rooms closing or changing their format. No longer was

Ronnie Schell autographed this photo to me and wife Erica. It modestly reads, "Best Wishes, Your Friend Ronnie Schell, One of the Truly Greats of Tomorrow."

there a demand for social and political satire. He went conventional, started playing the commercial rooms. He gave up making fun of the Teamsters, or offending Southern rednecks. For a while, it was said he had the funniest two-minute act in show biz. He built it back up again and became known as The Slowest Fastest Rising Young Comedian, a name given to him by San Francisco's most popular disc jockey of that period, Don Sherwood. The change must have been the right move, because he's been working popular clubs ever since. Let's also not forget that for five seasons (1964-

69) he portrayed a Marine named Duke on *Gomer Pyle - USMC*, at the side of his comedy pal, Jim Nabors, who had first created the Nabors hillbilly character on *The Andy Griffith Show*.

Ronnie is the kind of comedian who is funnier than his material. He has a style and a confidence in himself that compensates for only mildly amusing lines. Ronnie, then, falls into the personality category. What he says isn't much; it's all in the delivery and timing, and herein lies his success.

Backstage, with some of the first-show sweat still gleaming on his brow, Ronnie puffs on a giant cigar while he listens to these same opinions being put to him about his performance. He smiles and nods, not interrupting, just listening. He winks exaggeratedly at his bride of only a few days, Jan Rodeberg. She is a quiet woman who smiles demurely. Ronnie likes that. It makes up, he says, for his big mouth.

"Listen, what you've been saying is true," he finally replies, maneuvering the cigar in executive suite style. "Can you meet me for breakfast Saturday morning? We'll talk about the most important thing of all. Me." His eyebrows rise, fall, rise, fall. "And some other great funny people." Wink wink wink.

Saturday morning is misty, gray, spiritually depressing. Ronnie, dressed in a yellow-orange turtleneck, slacks, and topcoat, seems anything but depressed as he stands in front of the old, now-empty hungry i nightclub on Jackson Street. For years, it had been San Francisco's major showcase for all those comedians that had inspired Ronnie. Under the management of Enrico Banducci, it had been a breeding ground for the likes of Lenny Bruce, Mort Sahl, and Shelley Berman. Bill Cosby also got his start here in 1964, almost immediately becoming the star on a weekly TV series, *I Spy*. Also here at the hungry i, in 1963, Barbra Streisand performed as an unknown. Others over the years included Godfrey Cambridge, Professor Irwin Corey, Jonathan Winters, The Kingston Trio, and Dick Cavett.

Ronnie gazes through the smeared glass for a moment, then turns to look at the Purple Onion across the street, on Columbus. "That's where it started for me, back in '58, when owner Bud Steinhoff hired me at $85 a week. I moved over to the hungry i after I was making it big as really hot stuff. In fact, the first time I played the i was back in '59, the very night Jonnie [Jonathan] Winters went a little crazy and climbed the mast of the Balcutha. a ship docked over by Fisherman's Wharf." I've never forgotten what he shouted to the cops that night: 'Where am I from? I'm from outer space, man, outer space. I'm the man in the moon. I'm John Q. What's it to you?'

"Yeah, those were the golden days of nightclubs here in the city. I'd finish a show at the hungry i and jump into a cab so I could get to New Fack's in time to do another set with entirely different material."

Ronnie darts across Columbus Avenue and pauses in front of the Purple Onion, an intimate nightclub with steps leading down into a room where many entertainers got their start. On a marquee at the front door are listed those who were discovered there. Ronnie counts down to find his name positioned fifth, mingling with Phyllis Diller and Jim Nabors. He remembers back to those days. "What memories, just standing here, thinking about it all. Getting $85 a week to start. I was ecstatic. I loved every moment. Come on, we'll walk up to Enrico's for breakfast."

Enrico's is over on Broadway and named after the hungry i owner, Enrico Banducci. Although it hasn't officially opened yet, the head waiter recognizes Ronnie from earlier days and invites him to sit inside. Food will be available in about a half hour.

Ronnie slides into a booth and lights up a fresh cigar. "I consider a cigar my reward for honesty. And I just thought of myself as a great star." Ronnie is just a little more honest about himself as he explains he has only a small, supporting part opposite Jim Nabors on *Gomer Pyle - USMC*, a series running Friday nights on CBS. (However, it will last only a few more weeks, through early May.)

He explains, as his cigar weaves strange patterns through the air, "The series is based on two irregular guys against a normal world. Jim Nabors, a Marine private, and Frank Sutton, his sergeant. Everybody can't be a kook, so to balance that, they have someone sedate, sensitive, conservative. That's me, the Marine they call Duke. Duke Slater. Corporal to you." He beams proudly, stopping just long enough to take a drag on his cigar. "It's been good for me because I've learned about acting, about camera work. Not to mention four years of residuals. And I've never really complained because I've still had plenty of time to play clubs and concerts."

While Ronnie might have once been bitter over certain aspects of *Good Morning, World*, a 1967-1968 comedy series in which he starred (and which failed after just one season), he is now, at least on this dismal morning, jocund toward its demise. "They put us against the Tuesday night movies. So, somewhere in America every Tuesday night, thousands of men turned to thousands of wives and asked: 'Honey, do we watch Cary Grant or Ronnie Schell? So, our ratings were understandably not so high.

"Being so close to a show, it's hard to tell what went wrong. You might say the chemistry of the cast never jelled, say as it jelled for Andy Griffith or Dick Van Dyke. Perhaps it was the writing; some shows were clever; some not so clever."

Ronnie grows less flippant about his future in nightclubs. "I see the end of those clubs in sight. En toto. They're becoming an anachronism as we sit here, waiting for breakfast. As Enrico Banducci says, nightclubs are having a long funeral."

The waiter finally brings the morning *San Francisco Chronicle* and Ronnie, with the deftness of a bloodhound that has just picked up the scent, immediately turns to the entertainment section. He scans the review of his Bimbo show of two nights earlier, finding his name and uttering an erotic "Ah." He reads to himself. Finished, he makes a clicking noise. "Still haven't lost that old sex appeal of mine. Never will." He folds up the edition, seemingly pleased to the core.

At last, breakfast arrives, though it is more of a lunch: hamburger, melted cheese, a bun, and a little potato salad. Ronnie washes it all down with fruit juice, then leans back to contemplate his weaknesses as a performer. Of course, he'll be "totally honest" about that. "Laziness, that's my weakness. I always take the easy way out. You said it the other night—my material could be better. On the other hand, I'll spend all night to perfect a letter to an old friend, like Don Sherwood [San Francisco's most popular radio personality at the time.] But I vacillate. I'm schizoid. Went to a psychiatrist for two years, but couldn't do a thing to help him."

The lunch finished, Ronnie steps out onto Broadway. North Beach has yet to come alive, and the drizzle has increased slightly. He slips into his overcoat, thrusting his hands into its pockets. "The Street's changed since I played here last. Now it's almost nothing but Topless." What does he think of that trend? "I don't like it. It's only helped to kill legitimate entertainment, which is bad enough as it is. Say, where are you headed? Back to town? Oh . . . I think I'll walk down past the hungry i again. Probably be the only time I'll ever get over there. It's been great, John. Look me up when you're in L.A. covering stories.

"Come by my place at ten to eleven in the evening and we'll have a glass of Delaware Punch together. I have one every night at that time, after I've had my swim. We'll talk about the great comedians: W. C. Fields, Laurel and Hardy, Shecky Greene, Don Rickles." And, of course, Ronnie Schell.

Ronnie strides off down Kearny, toward Columbus. He passes a club advertising torrid topless dancers ("BOTTOMLESS! BOTTOMLESS!" proclaims a sign). His face says, "First no top? Now no bottom? Incredible!" He shakes his head bewilderingly, then hurries on.

Ronnie and I meet again in the summer of 1970 at Lake Tahoe, Nevada, where he and Jim Nabors are performing together at Harrah's Tahoe. Since our last rendezvous, Nabors has begun *The Jim Nabors Hour*, a variety series. Although they are old pals, sharing the stage, Schell is not a regular on the new series, and will be booked for only three episodes.

When I first see him, I think Ronnie is having a good night in the South Shore Room. Or is he? It depends on whose point of view you take. From a table in the showroom, which is packed with Fourth of July revelers, Ronnie seems in his best form—shotgunning his way through reams of material (and new material at that) like he has never done before, and carrying the whole thing with a degree of professionalism new even to the most devout of his fans.

From the point of view of the star of the show, Jim Nabors, Ronnie is firing them up all right, and his gay movie extra who breaks

Ronnie Schell

up the routine on an Audie Murphy movie set is a gem. Ronnie's still the funniest when it comes to self-destroying one-liners, but Ronnie doesn't seem to be having his usual fun. Nabors has seen enough of Ronnie's show to know if he is swinging with an audience or not, and tonight the comedian's just a bit up tight. That's how it looks to Jim Nabors.

Then there's Richard O. Linke, the show biz manager of both parties, and undoubtedly one of the television world's most fascinating wheeler-dealers. In Linke's book, you always kid a kidder, give him the needle, poke him in the ribs. So Linke's viewpoint is a flippant one, filled with pseudo-criticism (or so Ronnie hopes).

Ronnie's own point of view?

"Yeah, I was a little up tight tonight," he admits after the show, resting in Jim Nabors' dressing room. Ronnie has changed into the simple kind of clothes he used to wear at the hungry i and Purple Onion nightclubs (plain colored shirt with green sweater and khaki pants), and he still looks and acts like the kid from Richmond. With some people, stardom just never seems to go to their heads...

Jim Nabors has changed into a robe, and looks on the verge of exhaustion, which he is. He has been down with strep throat for about five days now, and in addition to missing two nights of his Las Vegas engagement, he had to delay the Harrah's opening by two nights.

That is the real reason Ronnie's so uptight. Normally called the second banana, or the supporting act, or the World's Slowest Rising Young Comedian, or the World's Fastest Slowest Rising Young Comedian, Ronnie suddenly found himself the headliner by default, and was supported the first night by comedienne Totie Fields ("with a girl her size, we both need support") and the second night by the singer, Rouvaun.

"Now you know why I was thrown," explains Ronnie. "I've just had to do three openings three nights in a row—with a totally different kind of audience each night. It makes it almost impossible to find your pace and confidence. And you know me when it comes to confidence." Ronnie shoves a thumb into his mouth and wraps an invisible security blanket around his body.

Nabors, meanwhile, takes a fistful of peanuts from a dish and begins to pop them, one at a time, into his mouth. He readjusts the towel wrapped around his neck.

"You need more rest," says manager Linke, pouring out a glass of coke for Jim. Jim polishes off the coke in three swallows and shoves more peanuts, one at a time, into his mouth. "You should maybe get more sleep at night," continues Linke, "and maybe bathe out in the sun for an hour in the afternoon. Do you good."

Nabors nods. "Yeah, I'm really beat."

Ronnie tells me that in a month he'll be playing either Caesar's Palace or the Frontier in Las Vegas. "The only thing I don't like about it all is, I never get to go home. And home is important to me, because I've got a newborn son, Gregory James Schell."

Dick Linke smiles and slaps Ronnie on the shoulder. "Zipperoonie."

Ronnie admits he has reached a level of show business that far surpasses any of his initial ambitions. "At first I just wanted to be a baseball player, and after surpassing that, I wanted to be a successful nightclub comedian. Of course, I was that years ago. So now I'm in a position of being far better and beyond anything I ever dreamed of."

Ronnie feels he has improved a great deal. "I really found my pace in Vegas, where I've appeared three times now. I've improved my timing." He wipes his fingernails on his sweater. "And everything else about me."

Forewarned that he has only another fifteen minutes before show time, Nabors loosens up his voice with a few practice singing notes, and excuses himself to change back into his white suit.

Ronnie, who must also change for the second show, pauses in the corridor outside. "Fame," he says, "there is plenty, but peace there is none." And he closes the door to his own dressing room.

I will not see Ronnie Schell again for the next seventeen years. And then . . .

There was something Ronnie Schell said during his appearance at Bimbo's 365 Club back in 1969: "I do vignettes. Vignettes have kept me out of the big time for years." Those words, in a way, seem prophetic in 1987 when applied to what Schell has accomplished over the past two decades. He has continued to splinter his career into "vignettes," accomplishing many things within the show-biz Big Time, but never becoming heavily identified with any hit movies or earthshaking TV series because of the smallness of his roles. Supporting player at best, never a star.

Yet the Schell Game works for Ronnie. He remains one of the busiest workaday character actors in Hollywood, turning out an unending stream of commercials, movies, TV shows, and personal

This is the front of a publicity postcard that Ronnie Schell sent to me after he saw my story in the San Francisco Chronicle.

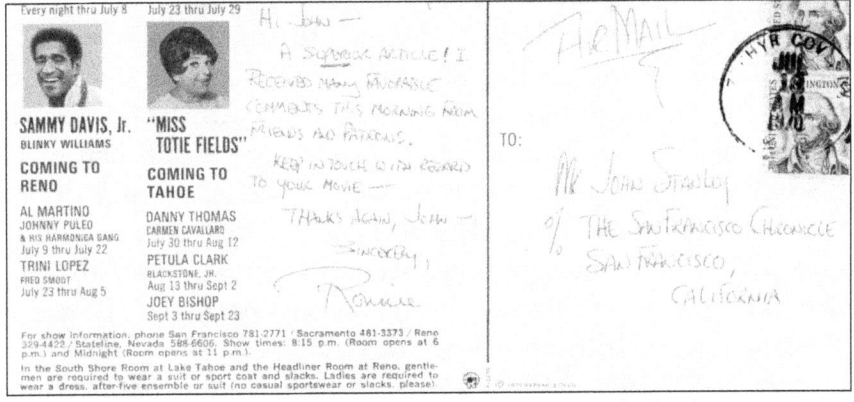

The backside of the publicity postcard from Ronnie Schell, who wrote: "Hi John – A superior article. I received many favorable comments this morning from friends and patrons. Keep in touch with regard to your movie. Thanks again, John. Ronnie." I think he was referring to my plan to make a feature film, which would not be completed until eight years later.

appearances. He isn't exactly set for life yet, but he concedes that he makes "a very good living," and has a number of assets, including buildings in Century City, Van Nuys, and Beverly Hills.

You used to see him as the national spokes-clown in TV commercials for Pacific Southwest Airlines. You've seen him for eighteen years as a character endorsing the San Francisco Giants for Channel 2 in the San Francisco-Bay Area. You can see him in Volkswagen commercials as the company's national spokes-humorist. You can see him in TV commercials for Shakey's Pizza (at least in some areas of California). You can see him portraying an angel in reruns of *Down to Earth* with Rip Taylor, and as a Marine named Duke in reruns of *Gomer Pyle - USMC*. You can hear his voice all the time on cartoon shows such as *The Smurfs, Ultraman, The Flintstone Kids,* and *Scubby Doo,* to name but a handful of titles. You can also see him doing his stand-up comedy act, a sharpened refinement of what he once did at the hungry i in the beatnik days of the 1950s and early 1960s, in the Pine Cone Lounge at the High Sierra Tahoe. See what I mean?

"Truthfully," Ronnie tells me during a visit to San Francisco, on the eve of his Tahoe opening, "I never had any ambition to be a big star. I just wanted to work, and it turned out quite well. My real ambition was to be successful in love and sex, and that turned out great."

It's nice that he hasn't lost any of his self-deprecation or his ability to make fun of himself when he's sitting in San Francisco's Bardelli's Restaurant, eating and reminiscing. Back in the 1950s, he used to sit at Enrico's on Broadway, often with radio's bon vivant, Don Sherwood, and watch the world parade past him.

For the first time, Ronnie tells me why he hadn't appeared more than three times on *The Jim Nabors Hour*, the follow-up to *Gomer Pyle - USMC*. "The happy bond between us ended when we both decided to work separately to explore new horizons." They are still good friends but don't see each other that often, now that Nabors lives in Hawaii tending to his macadamia nut orchards.

Those are dusty memories now, and Schell's wife of nearly twenty years, former schoolteacher Jan Roderberg, has told him to live in the present, never in the past, so he gets right to the present.

"I've just been signed for the Volkswagen commercials, of which there are now three sets of three each. It's good money, not earth-shaking. It's what I call 'generous.' And I won a Clio [the Emmy for advertising] for Kemp's Ice Cream. I almost melted."

If Ronnie has any heavy visible identity, he acknowledges that it comes from his commercials, which over the years have included such products as Goodrich, Honda, Schlitz Malt Liquor, Clorox, Wendy's, and Kelly-Moore, and which always showcase an element of his whimsical humor. "Today," he says, "a commercial is like a 30-second movie jimmy-wedged within a TV show. The programs live and die, come and go, but commercials keep going and people remember you more if you're a vignette than if you're the series' leading player.

"Commercials," he continues, "have the brightest directors in the business and often a lot of money is spent on them to make the product look as good as possible." Not to mention the actor. But don't call Ronnie the King of Commercials, reporting for duty each time a sponsor beckons. It doesn't happen that way. Not for Schell.

"I still have to audition ninety percent of the time. Only then does the sponsor see how great I am for the product. Once I've got the job, I'm usually asked to contribute to the humor, do some writing. I've even directed some radio commercials."

"These last seven years I've been traveling to conventions for IBM, playing this character named Garford C. Hogue and having a ball. He's this guy struggling to be the best for IBM, but not quite coming up to the standard." In addition, Schell has three films in the can. *Suds* is a comedy in which he's the boss of a Mexican resort; *Dutch Treat* is another comedy about a rock 'n roll group in Hollywood and he plays the head of Capitol Records. The third, *The Check Is in the Mail*, will remain in the can. "Mercifully," he adds.

Why do producers and sponsors keep choosing him? "I have all the ingredients for success," he replies with a grin. "Fine face, beautiful body, terrific timing, magnificent mind. All that aside, you need fiery ambition for stardom, and I've never quite had that kind of drive. To do comedy you have to be neurotic, insecure, anxious, maybe depressed. It's a burden most funny people have to live with. My priority, though, is happiness, and I've escaped the deep depression that some of my fellow comedians suffer from.

"I know too many who went after stardom and found it, only to discover they were still unhappy. Mainly because they still had this drive to succeed and had nothing to turn it onto. Frankly I don't know one well-adjusted star." As for his own vices, he confesses to "smoking a cigar on occasion, drinking three or four glasses of wine on the weekend, and taking a lot of afternoon naps."

Family is important to Ronnie, who says that having two sons (aged seventeen and twelve) "relieves anxieties. Would you believe I turned down an acting job recently so I wouldn't miss my son's little league game? Look, I'm making a good living, I'm respected by my peers, I have a nice reputation, and I've had only a few jobs I'm ashamed of. Not bad."

He looks robust and ruddy of face. "I still swim every night and work out one hour a day and jog about six miles. You have to, because the camera puts on the pounds. I stopped drinking Delaware Punch and now I take cranberry juice after my swim. And I don't eat meats; strictly chicken and fish."

Schell's current engagement at the High Sierra marks his first nightclub appearance in a while and prompted him to remark that he's probably "the last of the [hungry] i comics doing comedy. We all did comedy that was based on life and career. Our personal observations and witticisms. I look at the comedians today and I don't always know where they're coming from. What's their point of view? Some have great material, others don't. If I've had any success as a comedian it's because people identify me with life. I have things to say about what's going on in the world."

Inevitably, Ronnie can't stay out of the past too long, and as lunch ends, he returns to the topic of radio icon Don Sherwood, who had died in 1983 from emphysema at the age of fifty-eight. "The way we were," he muses, recalling the day long ago when he and Sherwood were going to be paid a lot of money for a job but instead went for a drive down to Ocean Beach. "When we arrived, Don pulled a revolver out of the cubbyhole and shot at the waves. He was getting an emotional release by taking it out on the Pacific Ocean. Don never saw himself as a talented person; he didn't have that drive I was talking about. He could have been a Johnny Carson; instead, he was pursued by personal demons. Monsters living within him. I was lucky. I kept the demons away." He sighs, and is back in the present again.

Ronnie Schell and I meet again in March 1988, at KTVU, the Oakland, California station where I had hosted *Creature Features* for six years. We are there to tape segments for a 30th anniversary celebration special, with Ronnie as the host. Tribute is paid to the news personnel and various personalities whom have hosted programs taped in the original studio at Jack London Square, then later at a new, far larger facility at Jack London Village, a short

That's me standing in the coffin my father had built as a prop for the feature film Nightmare in Blood, which I co-wrote, co-produced, and directed. Ronnie Schell, host of what would be called KTVU's 30th Anniversary Celebration, has just opened the lid to discover I have been waiting for him. I hand him a bottle of wine, then yawn and go back into the coffin, and act as if I'm about to fall asleep. This comedy bit was used in an opening segment collage.]

distance down the street. (Today, KTVU is an affiliate of the Fox Entertainment Network.)

March 1991. There is to be another major moment with Ronnie Schell.

He arrives back in the Bay Area to announce that he is the new media spokesman for the Bay Area Rapid Transit (BART), a rail system that runs exactly under our feet as we meet on Market Street, a block from the *San Francisco Chronicle* building. He excitedly tells me he is the replacement for Henny Youngman, the famous one-liner comedian. "They wanted someone born in the Bay Area, someone younger, and someone a lot funnier than Henny. I guess two out of three isn't too bad. It's always great to come back to where you got your start. I did my first commercial here for Taylor Topper Motor Scooters. The company sold seven."

Ronnie has now had ten years of spoofery in the name of Pacific Southeast Airline (PSA); having beer poured into his lap by Don Adams in Coors ads; selling Dodges from beneath a desk. It never stops for this kid from Richmond.

Take this comedian, please.

I contact Ronnie while preparing this book to discover that at the age of eighty-three, he is still busy as ever, still living happily with wife Janet in Los Angeles. "I'm still working Vegas twice a year," he tells me when we make contact. "When I go there in October it'll be my forty-ninth I do Lake Tahoe twice a year, too. Palm Springs every January, and a comedy room in Lincoln City, Oregon, once a year. And later this year I'll be working the Carnival Cruise Lines through the Caribbean as 'guest special entertainer.' I think I'm the only active comedian working the clubs except for my friend, Don Rickles. I'm still fooling them, John." And, he might have added, loving every moment.

Ronnie also tells me that his one-time agent Dick Linke is now in his nineties and living in Hawaii with his wife, Bettina. "He's in great shape and made a lot of money from *The Andy Griffith Show*, *Matlock* and *Gomer Pyle - USMC*. Speaking of rich, Jim Nabors still lives on a ranch on the island of Maui and I talk to him a couple of times a year. He rarely comes to California these days."

Ronnie Schell sent me this photo in July 2015, giving us insight into how he has conquered old age to still look young. He inscribed it with "John and Erica: I'm still fooling them! Love, Ronnie Schell 2015." Across his forehead Ronnie has written "Possibly a battle scar from the Korean War (Pusan 1952)." A little tongue-in-cheek commentary relating back to his Marine Corps days as Duke Slater (inset), a regular character on Gomer Pyle - USMC.

RICHARD KIEL (JAWS)
Sittin' & Jawin' With the Deadliest Villain Alive!
Nah, He's Just the Pussycat's Meow!

The man with the steel teeth walks across the dining room of the Hyatt on Union Square, dwarfing the six-foot-tall public relations executive walking meekly in his shadow. The Man With the Cobalt Jaw thuds noisily into a chair of dubious durability. The Unstoppable Human Target sinks an inch into foam before stopping. Oddly, the chair remains intact. Yet still he towers above the standing public relations man, who by now has begun to cringe.

On this day in August 1977, Jaws has arrived in San Francisco! And is he hungry for flesh! (At least it's not human flesh.) The waiters must hear the noises inside the Giant Tummy Bucket for they scurry like mice in several directions at once, devoted minions to please The Mighty Tall Man. Ah, so that's who he is: Jaws! The indestructible villain of the latest James Bond tomfoolery, *The Spy Who Loved Me*. Known to some humans existing on a slightly lower level as Richard Kiel. He has every right to dwarf other people.

In his stocking feet, he stands 7' 2" and might even be taller except for a slight hump in his back caused by cave dampness he picked up unexpectedly while portraying the titular Neanderthal man in *Eegah* (1961), his first feature film. Remember when the beautiful Marilyn Manning screamed her heart out each time he hovered into her line of sight? Remember how Arch Hall Jr. did his best to save the glamorous gal? Palm Springs, where the film was shot, has never been the same since.

Richard Kiel, let's see. He weighs in at 327 pounds, dresses in a 19-inch collar-sized shirt and wears a pair of shoes that sounds like a scream: 16EEE. Kiel's appetite for aforementioned flesh is omnivorous: He absorbs at least five meals a day to meet the growling (and ever growing?) demands of his innards—that's a full-course repeat every 4.8 hours. (Keep your watches wound as this interview begins!)

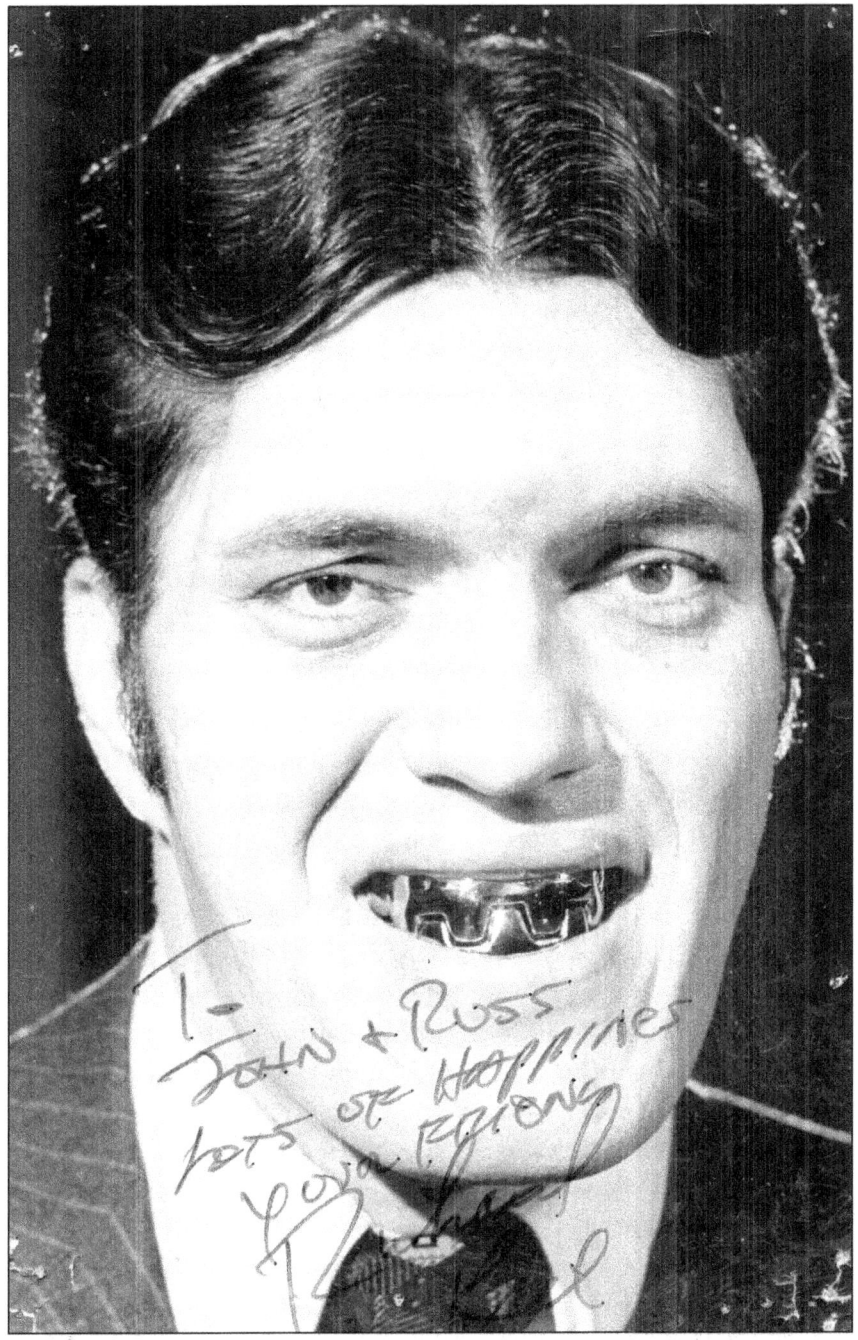

Richard Kiel closed his mouth just long enough to sign this The Spy Who Loved Me *publicity photo to me and my son Russ, followed by "Your friend, Richard Kiel."*

Richard Kiel in one of his menacing poses from The Spy Who Loved Me, *the film that will do more for his career than any other.*

Jaws, without a doubt, is one of the most indefatigable bad guys in movie history, and certainly in James Bond history. He uses his cobalt steel mouth to bite his victims in the neck a la Dracula. Bela Lugosi, were he alive, could learn a lot from Kiel; rather, from Jaws.

Look what he does in *The Spy Who Loved Me*: he survives the impact of a collapsing building (you could say he was floored several times). He single-handedly wrestles and puts the bite on a Great White Shark that sends the creature to the Lower Forty. (One can only wonder if Steven Spielberg intends to sue.) He is thrown from a speeding train and simply gets back on his feet, dusts off his jacket, and walks away. He certainly knows how to stay on track. He sustains a powerful electrical shock (his teeth acting as conductor). Finally, as he swims off into the sunset after surviving a savage underwater explosion, there still isn't a single mussed hair on his head. One wonders if he even required a make-up man during filming.

Like so many things bred and nurtured in Hollywood, Kiel's menacing presence and supposed brute force do not represent the inner man whom the public does not really know. For deep down inside, Richard Kiel is a pussycat. To prove it, he has brought along his wife and two children to our luncheon. He pats the kids on their heads in a fatherly fashion, and never glares nor gnashes his teeth at anyone as we sit and talk.

Kiel, who, according to legend, once had to be removed from the lavatory of a jetliner by a block and tackle, suffers from an overactive pituitary gland, and apparently suffers inwardly at the mere direct mention or subtle suggestion of physical violence.

The former door-to-door salesman for cemetery plots (I am not kidding!) places his massive hands on the table, and I would swear it shakes just a little. "These are strong," he says, with some sense of pride. "But, I hate to use force. Have ever since I was a kid growing up in Detroit, where it was impossible for me to find any dancing partners.

"I've been a bouncer in a North Hollywood nightclub but I never liked to fight, so I'd always come on like some kind of crazy. That scared people and they'd instantly pull back and apologize, or just turn and run for the front door. Usually they galloped at full speed. Then the trouble was over and I could go back to being a nice strong-arm door man."

Coming on like a crazy has kept Kiel busy in motion pictures and TV for seventeen years. He's worn the funny monster suits; he's worked opposite dwarf Michael Dunn on *The Wild, Wild West* portraying Dr. Miguelito Loveless' henchman, Voltaire; and he's been a regular on *Barbary Coast* (fourteen episodes as the bouncer aptly named Moose Moran). He's bashed noggins and furniture with equal ease, and he's flipped over an occasional diesel truck with one arm tied behind his back. "Without spilling any gas," he adds.

He confesses to me that *The Spy Who Loved Me* is the highpoint of his acting career, even though he doesn't utter a single line of dialogue. Grunts and groans, he adds, don't count.

"Most of my other films have been cheap horror programmers [*The Phantom Planet*] or low-budget quickies—quick in regard to how quick people forget them." He would like to forget them too, but *The Human Duplicators, The Nasty Rabbit, House of the*

Damned, and *Flash and the Firecat* keep coming back to work him over on The Late Show. (His roles in *The Longest Yard* and *Silver Streak*, he likes better.)

Kiel has been talking frequently with Bond producer Albert Broccoli about the possibility of Jaws returning in the next Bond escapade. After all, he was not killed . . . yet. "So far, it's just talk, but I'm hopeful because audiences have enjoyed the character. No one takes him too seriously; everyone knows these films are designed to be tongue-in-cheek. I tried to make something special of Jaws and I hope that extra effort will lead to more work and more meaningful roles. I'd like producers to think of me as a normal actor who just happens to be a little taller than most folks."

Richard Kiel's wish to play Jaws again came true two years later in the James Bond thriller, *Moonraker*. Also in 2003, he provided the voice of Jaws for the video game *James Bond 007: Everything or Nothing*. Unfortunately, a car accident he endured in 1992 resulted in a loss of balance and the need for a cane. In 2002, his autobiography, *Making It Big in the Movies*, revealed that he suffered from a fear of heights, and hence, a stunt double was used in the scenes where he was standing atop a cable car high in the sky. He died in 2014 just a few days short of his seventy-fifth birthday.

One final look at Richard Kiel as Jaws. I will always remember it as lunch with a crunch. The irony of it all: he seemed like the sweetest guy around when you sat down to talk to him. Isn't life ironic?

CHUCK JONES
Mr. Jones Went to Warner Bros. To Help Create a Funny Bunny –But That's Not All, Folks

How do you greet an artist who helped give Bugs Bunny his loveable "What's Up, Doc?" personality, who created Pepe Le Pew's odoriferous attitude, who gave the Road Runner his speedy *savior-faire*, and who gave Wile E. Coyote his bottomless appetite?

When Chuck Jones strides across the threshold, one simply says "Beep beep," and five decades of Warner Bros. cartoons have been heralded.

The door that Jones comes through in November 1989 is at Circle Gallery in San Francisco's Ghirardelli Square, where reproductions of his sketches of some of the beloved Warner Bros. characters are on exhibit for a few hours before going on sale.

Chuck Jones' 1989 publicity photo, designed to help sell his new book, Chuck Amuck, the history of Warner Bros. cartoons and Jones' contributions. Just in case you didn't recognize them, the creature at right is the Road Runner.

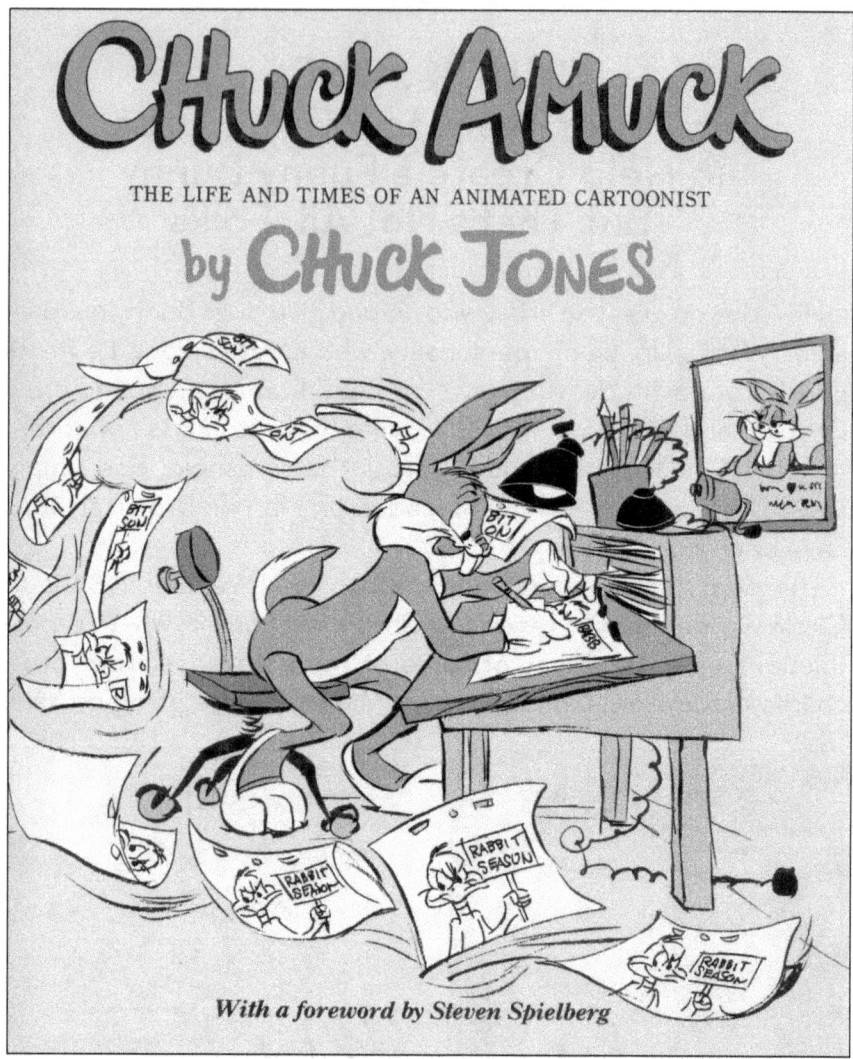

The cover of Chuck Jones' autobiography, which details the making of such Warner Bros. classics as For Scentimental Reasons *and* What's Opera, Doc?

Here, a Pepe Le Pew; there, a Daffy Duck. Is that Marvin Martian over there next to Henry Hawk, who's next to Porky Pig? Also, isn't that Bugs sketch in which he's munching on a carrot cute?

In a stroke of parody, Jones also has a series of lithographs that integrate the famous Warner Bros. cartoon characters into pastiches of the old masters: Wile E. Coyote in a Van Gogh pose, a "nude" Daffy descending a staircase, a rendering of a Paris duck with top hat and cane like Toulouse-Lautrec.

The title page of Chuck Jones' book, on which he took time to draw images of Wile E. Coyote and the Road Runner, just for me. Inscription: "For John from Wile E. Coyote & Chuck Jones & The Road Runner. 11/30/89"

When Chuck Jones' art goes on sale, it goes fast. "Within forty-eight hours," a gallery employee remarks, "the walls will be as barren as Wile E. Coyote's Road Runner meat supply."

Jones, at the age of seventy-seven, is an American master animator, to whom history has paid homage in his own lifetime. He is among the last surviving representatives of the Golden Age of cartooning, when the art form was still being shaped in a spirit of maverick innovation. *Time* magazine once described him as a man "who had made moviegoers laugh as often and as well as Buster Keaton or Charlie Chaplin."

When Jones and his collaborators were turning out the Warner Bros. cartoons during the 1930s and 1940s, "we thought we were making them for movie theaters," Jones recalls. "We thought they were dispensable, to be shown briefly and then retired to the vaults. We certainly never dreamed they had any social significance. We didn't dream of television existing, and we never dreamed these characters had a life of their own that would carry them on and on, far beyond the life spans of those of us who created them. One day I'll be gone, but Bugs Bunny . . . he'll be forever."

Television and written history have given those mini-masterpieces of animation a longevity that one assumes could be everlasting. Warner Bros. cartoons were produced in an air of iconoclastic disregard for the front office that was footing the bills. Jones and his acolytes were making cartoons mainly for themselves and their own peculiar senses of humor. The cartoons are as beloved as ever, having lost none of their zany humor or zippy characters. If anything, in an era when there are fewer and fewer "fully animated" works, they seem to get tastier with age.

Now Jones has added to his own iconography with *Chuck Amuck*, a collection of bemused memoirs (subtitled *The Life and Times of an Animated Cartoonist*) that traces not only the history of Bugs Bunny and the gang but of those who designed them—down to the alcoholic handyman, Smokey Garner, who used to sweep out the studio each night.

Seated in a small room, its walls covered with a selection of cartoon reproductions, Jones sips a soft drink and looks very much the academician in a herringbone tweed jacket, gray shirt, and bow tie. Pondering the continuing success of Bugs Bunny, Jones tells me, "Once an old lady said to me, 'I can't understand why you're writing scripts for Bugs Bunny. He's funny enough just as he is.' Then there was the boy to whom I was introduced as the man who drew Bugs Bunny. The boy shook his head and said, 'He draws pictures of Bugs Bunny.'

"In both cases, they believed in Bugs, and that's the key to the success of the series. It isn't the drawing that makes the character, or the voice. It all hinges on how the character moves. We are the way we move. Out of movement comes solidity and balance—and believability. There's nothing less believable to a child than a marionette that doesn't quite touch the ground and hops along in midair. Bugs' stance—his weight on one leg, the other leg casually crossed—was inspired by actor George Sanders as he held a chicken wing in the film, *Rebecca*. Believability gets you sympathy, and you need sympathy because without it you can't be funny. Life itself is not funny; it's the incongruities that are funny. 'What's up, Doc?' is funny only in Bugs' own environment."

As artists, Jones continues, "we always believed in Bugs as a consistent personality. We liked our characters, we never mocked them. I'd come home at night and say to my daughter, 'Know what Daffy Duck said to me today?' Because those characters did speak to us—sometimes the most unexpected things. Out of happy accidents came new ideas. You must always go inside yourself to do character. George Orwell once said, 'I never met a man worse than I am.'

"Character is all that matters in the making of great comedians-in animation and live action. And good characters are based on variations of observable human behavior."

Take, for example, Groucho and Chico Marx. "Each had his own style," points out Jones. "So do Bugs and Daffy. Bugs always gets into trouble because he's been provoked by predators. Daffy Duck always gets into trouble because of his own ego. Bugs talks, but Daffy talks too much. So you see, even within chaotic, bizarre events, each character has a point of view, a solid ground to stand on."

Even within the lunatic landscape of Wile E. Coyote and the Road Runner, Jones insists, "there are rules, such as: The devices from the Acme Co. never work, and Coyote never questions their credibility. Such as, Coyote is always more humiliated than harmed by his failures. Such as, Coyote can run on empty air as long as he doesn't realize he's not on the ground. Such as, Coyote could stop anytime, if he wasn't such a fanatic. As George Santayana once said, 'A fanatic is one who redoubles his effort when he has forgotten his aim.' Coyote is a multiplication of us all. We're all familiar with making mistakes and failure. We've all felt humiliation."

Jones' success as an animator was preceded by his abject failure as a commercial artist. He began by dropping out of high school to attend the Chouinard Art Institute in Los Angeles. He claims to have graduated "without distinction or the ability to draw." Hence his early career disasters. Ten years of night school followed, but it still didn't prevent him from failing in the commercial market. ("I still could not draw but could now fake it fairly well.")

A cell washer was a low-on-the-totem-pole worker in those days, but Jones was considered well-suited to it by Ub Iwerks, a pioneer animator, who had left Walt Disney to start his own company. Jones worked in all the menial positions as cel painter, cel inker, and "in-betweener," or assistant director, before he was fired by Iwerks—not once but twice.

In 1933, fortunately for the history of animation, Jones went to work for Leon Schlesinger, a hard-driving businessman who knew little about cartoons but a lot about saving a buck when it came to providing Warner Bros. with a series of *Looney Tunes* cartoons. These were made independently, off the main lot, in a falling-down place called Termite Terrace.

It was under the regime of the less-than-lovable Schlesinger (whose lisp was to inspire Daffy Duck's) that Jones "finally" learned how to draw and began "fumbling around" with the art of animation while rubbing shoulders with Tex Avery, Isadore (Friz) Freleng, Bob Clampett, Frank Tashlin, and Robert McKimson, all of whom went on to establish successful careers at Warner Bros. (Tashlin even went on to become a feature film director.)

"Bugs Bunny was bustin' out all over," Jones recalls. He didn't create Bugs but he helped to shape his best traits. Although he went on to create thirteen characters for the series, the most endearing ones turned out to be Pepe Le Pew, Wile E. Coyote, and the Road Runner.

From 1934 until 1963, when Warner Bros. closed down its animation studio, Jones was involved in making 221 cartoons. Among them were some gems: *Duck Amuck* is still one of the best of the

Daffy cartoons in which he battles with the very animators who created him; *Duck Dodgers in the 24 · Century,* a masterful parody of the science-fiction comic strip *Buck Rogers; What's Opera, Doc?,* a satire on Wagner's "Ring of the Nibelungen"; and *One Froggy Evening,* the riotous tale of Michigan J. Frog, a creature capable of singing "Hello, My Baby" in top hat and tails.

Jones was upset about "having Warner pulled out from under me," and says it happened after he and his wife had written the script for the animated feature *Gay Purr-ee,* about cats living in Paris. "Because I had an exclusive contract with Warner Bros., Jack L. Warner decided to fire me. But, I moved on to good things. *Tom and Jerry* shorts for MGM, Dr. Seuss' *How the Grinch Stole Christmas* and *Horton Hears a Who.* Plus there was a feature, *The Phantom Toolbooth.*"

During his fifty years as an animator, Chuck Jones won three Oscars and hundreds of other honors and awards. He has also returned to the Warner Bros. fold to produce special compilations of the old cartoons with new wraparound footage.

"I was lucky," he says. "For sixty years someone was willing to pay me to draw. We never did the chapter Saturday-morning style of animation. We always did it the right way. The full way. The only way."

He isn't finished with Warner Bros. There are always half-a-dozen TV projects on his drawing board. As for the time spent between me and Chuck Jones, there will be one more encounter, meaning that's not all, folks.

I will sit with Chuck Jones one more time, two years later. In summer 1991, he returns to San Francisco and stakes himself out at the Owl Gallery to sell hand-signed lithographs and limited edition cartoon cells. Later, in his St. Francis Hotel suite, he sketches an exclusive portrait of Bugs Bunny, autographs it, and turns it over to me. Then, he tells me that his old cartoons are being shown in the form of music concerts entitled Bugs Bunny on Broadway. The cartoons are projected on stage while George Daugherty conducts the 50-piece Warner Bros. Symphony Orchestra, re-creating the musical soundtracks originally composed by Carl Stalling and orchestrated by Milton Franklyn.

This is the original Bugs Bunny sketch Chuck Jones drew during our second rendezvous. It was his way of telling me that a live music show featuring Warner Bros. cartoon characters, Bugs Bunny on Broadway, would soon be playing in the San Francisco Bay Area. It's dated 7/17/91.

"The amazing thing," Jones tells me, "is that we never made them for children. We didn't sit around discussing demographics. If something was funny, if we laughed during the story session, it was enough to satisfy us. Because we didn't compromise anything, because the material was flowing out of us, the cartoons turned out reasonably sophisticated."

Jones also admits to me he has always admired Carl Stalling's scores. "Carl could take the most sacred music, Mozart for example, for a Wile E. Coyote sequence, and speed it up until you couldn't recognize it. Or he could take Offenbach and slow it way, way down and it would become an elephant's walk. Carl used to astonish me with each new score, and now, with this new music show, I'm astonished all over again. Carl has been dead for many years, but in my heart it's as if he was back to life again. And I'm enjoying it in a new way."

Chuck Jones stayed very busy for the remaining ten years of his life. He directed animated sequences in *Stay Tuned* (1992) and *Mrs. Doubtfire* (1993). His final cartoon was to be *From Hare to Eternity* (1996), starring the one and only Bugs Bunny. Jones died of a heart attack in 2002.

TOM HANKS
What a Drag... Wait! Holy Baloney! It's Tom Hanks in 'Bosom Buddies'

Given where Tom Hanks was in April 1981, when we met at KGO-TV in San Francisco, I had no idea he would rise up through the ranks of Hollywood to become not only a major film star but a producer of some excellent documentaries and dramatic re-enactments of World War II. For the moment, he was still "busting" into the business with an unprecedented drive to succeed.

Tom buys his clothes exclusively at Blouse City: pink frilly blouses, spiked high heels, and pleated skirts. Undergarments? Now you're getting a little too personal. Frankly, he is getting just a little fed up with people who ask about his bra and pantyhose sizes. Dare we say he thinks the whole business is a "drag"?

Tom's career started when producers Tom Miller, Ed Milkis, and Bob Boyett called him in a year ago to audition for a new sitcom. "Did he object to wearing women's clothing?" they asked discreetly, when nobody else was listening. "Were his ankles so ugly he'd look lousy in high heels?" they queried with tact and subtlety. Tom, who isn't even sure how to spell transvestite, shook his head.

"No, no objection," Tom told Miller/Milklis/Boyett, not if it meant playing a role on TV and earning some dough. Emphasis on the money. He was in debt to a lot of his friends and he had a family to support. Who's going to get particular at a time like now?

The role turned out to be two: hard-working, struggling commercial artist Kip Wilson (employed by a New York advertising agency) who, in sexual turnabout, was Buffy, a soft-voiced, less-than-pretty, sometimes bumbling young brunette rushing in and out of the all-women's Susan B. Anthony Hotel. Something odd about that girl, but of course no one can ever quite put their figure on it.

The comedy series, *Bosom Buddies*, premiered in the fall of 1980 with what sounded like a one-shot gimmick: two Madison Avenue advertising figures pose as women as part of their subterfuge to

Tom Hanks during his early years when he was still struggling to hit the Big Time in the TV/movie business.

maintain cheap living quarters. Why do they have to be cheap? Don't ask. Just strip your mind of logic and let things flow along.

These two red-blooded American males don't want to take advantage of a blonde bombshell (Donna Dixon), spy on the va-va-voom girls when they are undressing, or be in close proximity to cop a free feel. They just want to have a few hard-earned bucks remain in their wallets, that's all. Hey, pal, these are tough inflationary times.

Understandably, TV critics came down hard on *Bosom Buddies* for the padding of its humor ("Are they crooked?" one buddy asks another as he adjusts his falsies) and the scrawniness of its form. As *San Francisco Chronicle* TV critic Terence O'Flaherty wrote, "The best thing about *Bosom Buddies* is that it doesn't take place in San Francisco."

Going drag is a shtick that worked like a jawbreaker for *Charlie's Aunt*, which broke all records on the London stage in the 1890s, and served as a Jack Benny film vehicle in 1941. Drag also worked for Jack Lemmon and Tony Curtis in the context of that zany Billy Wilder comedy *Some Like It Hot* (1959). In more modern times, it served well for the character of Klinger on *M*A*S*H*.

How could drag be sustained in a sitcom week in and week out? Well, it sort of worked for Peter Kastner when he tried it in a 1968 comedy series, *The Ugliest Girl in Town*. Critics guessed that his falsies would become instantly deflated. The viewing public, to the surprise of critics that predicted early cancellation, seemed to accept the shtick and tuned in often enough to keep the program among the Top 20 shows.

For Tom Hanks, the drag shtick is beginning to irritate him, and, frankly, he now finds it embarrassing when the original photographs of him and his co-star Peter Scolari (playing Henry Desmond/Hildegard) are brought out as examples of their non-ravishing "look." That really isn't what it's all about, he says defensively, pointing out that many of the scripts shied away completely from the drag theme and others had only a minimum of scenes requiring the brunette wig and female apparel. These, he stresses, were the strongest episodes.

"To my way of thinking," says Tom, "there's nothing funny about two guys posing as girls after nineteen episodes. How can you still be fresh and unique? It hasn't become painful or pedestrian yet. But in the long run—and the long run is always the final yardstick for success—we'll have to look for another aspect."

Tom thinks that aspect might be pursuing the professional and personal lives of the two main characters that are constantly compromising their ideals to keep their jobs but without the drag gimmick. That would require *Bosom Buddies* to become *Biceps Brothers.*

According to Tom, there has been a dialogue between cast and producers all winter long about this very problem. ABC has "unofficially" given its approval to a second season depicting the misadventures of Kip Wilson and Henry Desmond.

Tom, now twenty-five, is a native of the Bay Area and was born in Concord. His father was active in the restaurant business, and young Tom grew up washing dishes and stuffing potatoes in tinfoil in such places as the Sea Wolf and Castaways in Oakland. He moved around a lot, and his mother and father went through divorce, but he loved hanging around restaurants and recalls that it was a happy childhood.

While attending Chabot College in Hayward, he attended dozens of plays to research a paper he was writing. One night, from a cheap seat in the balcony, he was electrified by O'Neill's *The Iceman Cometh.* "It was an incredible evening which I'll never forget. I was mesmerized and swept away. Theater solidified all my energies. From that moment forth, I vowed to dedicate my life to acting."

Tom went to Sacramento State but admits he was only "goofing around in the Theater Arts Department. I really wasn't going to college." He never came near graduating; instead he worked for the Sacramento Civic Theater, then transferred to the Great Lakes Shakespeare Festival in Cleveland where he served as an intern ("I did all the dirty work backstage.")

In going back and forth between Sacramento and Cleveland, he earned his first important stage roles and met a kindred soul in theater, actress Samantha Lewes. They fell hopelessly in love. Samantha bore him a son three years ago but they have been married for less than two years. A second child is on the way. "We were children of the 1970s," says Hanks, shrugging.

In 1978, they moved to New York, where Hanks underwent a career trauma. "New York frightened and excited me in the same breath. I wanted only to stay in bed, drink coffee, and avoid the terrible crush outside. Like the world was closing in on me. I wouldn't go outside for days. I had to re-psyche myself up before I could make the rounds to see agents. For six months, Samantha and I were penniless. We'd eat Cream O' Wheat so our baby could be fed."

It took Hanks nearly a year to make a modicum of headway. He was cast in *The Mandrake* off-off Broadway and then did a small role in a psycho-killer flick, *He Knows You're Alone*, which today he describes as a film "about a moron slashing up brides. There was nothing redeeming about it. It was just a job."

Tom was doing *The Taming of the Shrew* with the Riverside Shakespeare Company when ABC began holding interviews with young "hopefuls."

"Nobody ever told me what was going on. I made three trips out to the West Coast and went through tests and auditions. ABC had promised to reimburse me, but first I had to get and spend the money and that wasn't so easy. I borrowed all I could from friends."

There followed several meetings with producers. He tried out for the leading role in *Foul Play* but he knew he wasn't right for the part. Just as well because the series came and went. When he walked into the clutches of the *Bosom Buddies* producers, he was literally flat broke and on the verge of desperation.

Career fortune came so fast in his life that he realizes now he has to insulate himself against the dangers of too much too soon. "I think I have my feet firmly on the ground. I still look upon myself as a journeyman actor with 2,002 different roles and 2,002 different things I want to achieve. I just hope I get the opportunity to play a few of them."

Tom was to get his wish. The door to the world of movies would soon open up to him. Although *Bosom Buddies* lasted only two seasons, word got around about his acting talents, and he be-

Tom Hanks in Bachelor Party (1984).   Tom Hanks in Big (1988).

gan making feature films. A major upswing in his career came with *Bachelor Party* (1984), *Nothing in Common* (1986) opposite Jackie Gleason, and a comedy version of *Dragnet* (1987) costarring Dan Aykroyd. *Big* (1988) made money and turned him into a major player. *Joe vs. the Volcano* (1990) and *A League of Their Own* (1992) were followed by *Philadelphia* (1992), in which he portrayed a gay attorney dying of AIDS. The role brought him an Oscar for Best Actor.

I am to enjoy a second sit-down meeting with Tom in the summer of 1993 to talk about *Sleepless in Seattle*, in which he portrays a grieving husband recovering from the trauma of losing his wife and having to raise an eight-year-old alone.

When I ask him about his constant rise to stardom ever since the passing of *Bosom Buddies*, he bursts out laughing, displaying an almost devil-may-care openness about his career. "This is such a fragile world, this business of making movies, that I often reel myself in and step back to look at things carefully, as objectively as I can. I had to make five or six pictures before I figured out what the hell I was doing. I guess it was after *Big*, in which I got to play

Tom Hanks in Joe Vs the Volcano *(1990).*

a boy in a man's body, that I sat down and saw my work. I saw that it was good and that *Big* worked on a level none of my other films had quite worked on. And I was somewhere new. And then you do something like *A League of Their Own*, where you kind of make fun of your screen image, and you're somewhere else new again.

And now I've played a gay lawyer in *Philadelphia*, which is as far removed from anything I've ever done. No, I had no trepidations about playing that role. I never had to manufacture a choice, or rationalize why I should play the character. The material was top-

Tom Hanks signed this photo from The Man in One Red Shoe *(made in 1985) on the day we met in Hollywood to talk about* Sleepless in Seattle. *"John and Erica, God Bless, Tom Hanks"*

notch, one of those rare good scripts I was describing. That was all I needed to know that I wanted to do it. You don't pass up a good part like that."

He laughs again, bemused by the universe circling around him. "It's crazy, this movie business, but it's wonderful. And even though the risks are always there, God bless America."

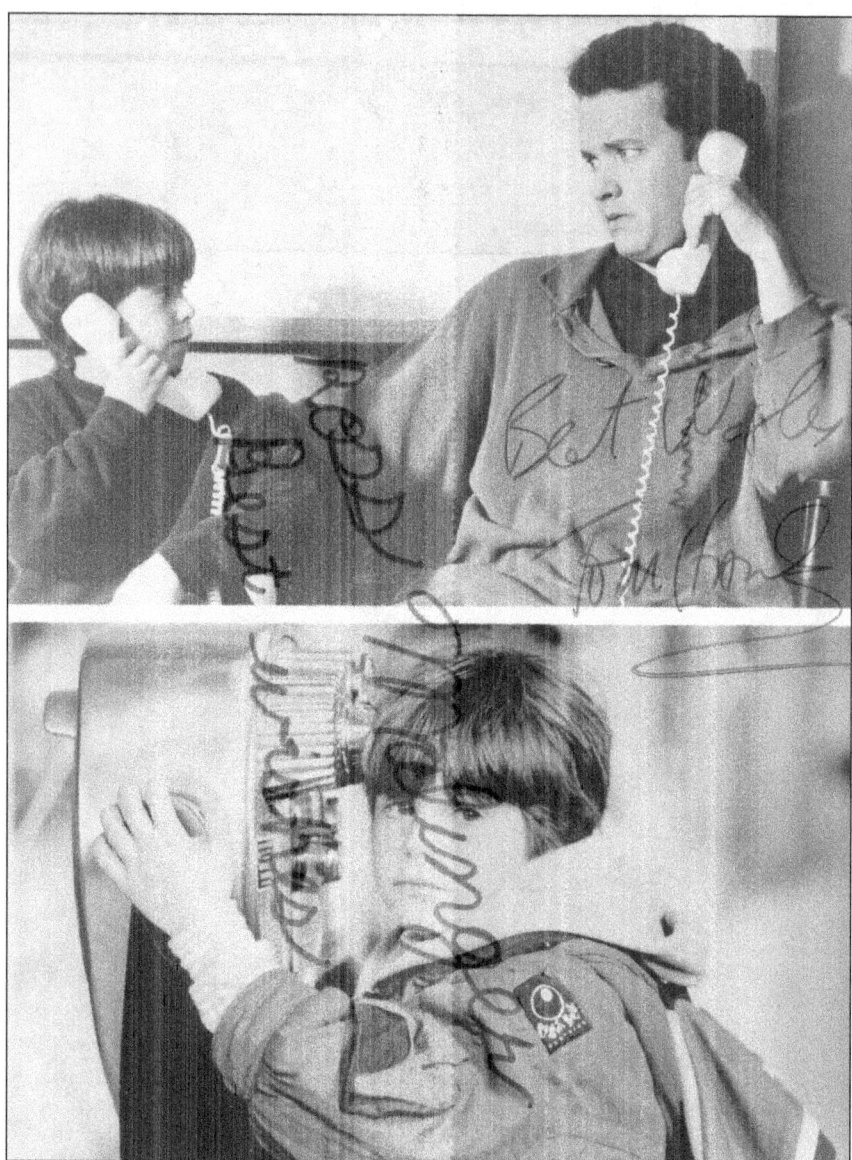

This Sleepless in Seattle *photo was signed by both Tom Hanks and Ross Malinger, who portrays Hanks' son in the Nora Ephron-directed romance.*

Tom Hanks' success in Hollywood has never let up, and he's displayed remarkable talent as a producer. He joined with Steven Spielberg to make *Saving Private Ryan* (2001), considered a superior World War II film, and that led to him producing and directing *Band of Brothers* (dramatized events of the war in Europe),

Another signed Tom Hanks photo, this one to my son Russ. "God Bless, Tom Hanks."

and later producing a series about the Marine Corps in World War II, *The Pacific*.

In terms of acting, he's recently scored big in *Captain Phillips* and *Saving Mrs. Banks*. Both reveal his all-around talents as actor. Back in 1981, given *Bosom Buddies,* who could have known?

CAROL BURNETT
Get a Load of the Chu Chu: It's Burnett in 'Early Tacky' In the City's Finest Hotel

Atop Nob Hill, on the third floor of the Fairmont Hotel in Room 380, Carol Burnett sits on an unmade bed, looking completely made up. Throwing both legs into the air at once, she rotates one multi-colored spike heel toward my throat as if it were a lethal weapon. Her legs in nylon dominate the altitude around me and are as slender as the rest of Carol . . . nice-looking for a woman who is forty-five.

The high heels are no crazier than the rest of Carol's outfit, what she describes as "early tacky." There's a tight-fitting burgundy print dress with a huge opening just above the belly button. That turns the top-half into a bra halter that is working overtime to contain itself. Over the vulgar dress is a less vulgar coral housecoat,

Carol Burnett as street dancer Chu Chu in *Chu Chu and the Philly Flash,* her 1981 comedy made on location in San Francisco.

unbuttoned for full exposure, with rhinestone and pearl studs on the collar. Finally, draped over the housecoat in the style of a flapper is a lavender scarf.

Get a load of the jewelry. On one hand, an emerald jeweled bracelet, a red wristband with white watch, and a heart-shaped ring. On her other hand, a rectangular rhinestone ring with at least two rhinestones missing. Topping it all off is a red curly wig atop which is perched a burgundy corduroy tam. Whew! On the other hand, I'm wearing nothing but a plain old suit and tie—Mr. Ordinary meeting a TV comedy star of the 1970s, who is now starring in a movie made in San Francisco.

"If you think this is something," Carol tells me, "you should see my Carmen Miranda outfit. Halter bolero with tassels and sequins, a wraparound skirt with a cowbell in front and a bull's-eye panted on the rear. And my six-inch platform heels painted with bananas and other fruits." Definitely tutti-frutti.

Carol Burnett comes on like a lady selling zest by the pound. She's chatty, charming, and, obviously, having a ball playing one of life's gaudy misfits in the comedy *Chu Chu and the Philly Flash*, a Mel Simon production now being shot in the month of October 1980.

"A thrill I am having," she says, ignoring the commotion out in the corridor as director David Lowell Rich prepares another camera set-up. "Chu Chu is my kind of girl. A street performer who's terrible. A sweet kid who dresses like Carmen Miranda when she performs on the street. She's a one-woman band. Uke, harmonica, motorized drums—this girl who thinks she has everything. The truth? She has nothing when it comes to talent. She dreams of being a super supper club singer but you know she'll never make through the front door, let alone reach the stage."

On, on went Carol: "And The Philly Flash? Alan Arkin looking wonderfully like a bum. And what a character. He's a down-and-out baseball player. Formerly with the Philadelphia Phillies. He pitched relief one day, back in 1957, and that's been his only moment of glory since. Now he's hanging out with some derelicts and street folk, trying to get enough money together through various scams so he can get to Michigan where there's an umpire's job waiting. That's when we meet and become a serious number."

Carol Burnett with costar Alan Arkin, sprawled out on a San Francisco street in a publicity photo for Chu Chu and the Philly Flash.

As if to live up to Carol's description, Alan Arkin shuffles past Room 380, almost unrecognizable in a grungy raincoat, a red Phillipe cap, and scruffy pants that bag at his feet. The make-up team has done such a fine job of dropping him to Skid Row status that in the South of Market area he'd be the creme de la creme of gutter society.

Chu Chu and the Philly Flash was originally written by Bob Merrill to be a caper movie. When Arkin read the screenplay, he liked the character but not the heist business and decided to buy the property and have it rewritten to suit his own talents. He gave that job to his wife of sixteen years, Barbara Dana, who threw out most of Merrill's concept and turned it into a character/relationship story with the caper elements minimized. Still, it's described by unit publicist Susan Alschuler as "a hilarious adventure that leads to blackmail, kidnapping, a potential murder . . . and love."

Carol stresses only the love interest between Emily (Chu Chu) and the Philly. "We're madly, passionately getting it on. Yet there's enough friction to cause catfights. We're bigger than life but we're still believable."

It hasn't all been comedy in Carol's personal life these past few years. The current issue of *Ladies' Home Journal* has a story she wrote recounting the ordeal with her daughter, Carrie, who was discovered to be a drug addict at the age of thirteen. The sub-

Carol Burnett as a failed entertainer trying to rejuvenate her life and romance with a former baseball star (Alan Arkin) in Chu Chu and the Philly Flash.

ject seems a natural and topical one for discussion, but Carol has made it clear beforehand that this is one arena she doesn't want to leap into.

Her spangled costume notwithstanding, Carol has had less exposure since giving up her weekly CBS-TV series (after an eleven-year run) in April 1978. In Carol's case, this was her own decision. "I wanted to quit before someone told me the show was cancelled. It happens sooner or later to everyone in TV. It was a graceful way to bow out while everyone's thoughts were still positive.

"Yes, I missed the show at first. But more, I missed my second family, my studio family. I began to get the bends after not seeing Tim Conway for a week. I'd lived with the deaths, births, marriages, and divorces of those around me. I'd seen people grow up before my eyes during those eleven years. But after a while, I got over it and began to enjoy my own family again.

"I'll never go back to a weekly series. You should never do something you've already done. Even if it's better, people have a way of glancing back and comparing it and deciding it's never as good as 'the Good Old Days.' It's human nature to wax nostalgically."

Another major reason for leaving TV was her wish to do more dramatic acting. She answered that need by making three TV

Rita Hayworth and Carol Burnett performing a comedy sketch during Burnett's long-running CBS variety/comedy series.

movies back-to-back in 1978-1979. In *Friendly Fire*, she was the grief-stricken mother of a young man killed in Vietnam by his own artillery; in *The Tenth Month*, she was a divorcee who became pregnant and decided to have her baby even though the father was married; and in *The Grass Is Greener Over the Septic Tank*, she slipped back into her role as mirth-maker, having a ball as a wacky housewife. In the scheme of TV, these were all prestigious shows and they elevated her to a new eminence among producers seeking a dramatic actress.

Carol's train of thought is interrupted by director Rich, who waves her into the hallway for the next scene. She's handed a briefcase that contains precious paperwork everyone in the plot is chasing after—what Alfred Hitchcock would call the McGuffin. After two rehearsals the camera is set to roll. Action! . . . Carol and Arkin stroll along the corridor toward Room 380. Arkin lifts his hand to knock when suddenly the door flies open and three actors—cast costar Danny Aiello and San Francisco extra stalwarts Scott Beach and Morgan Upton—come flying out. (I undergo an utterly personal surprise at this moment because I know Morgan firsthand. A few years earlier, I had chosen him to portray a TV horror host in my film *Nightmare in Blood*. He proved to be delightfully amusing, and he carried that same sense of humor as he popped into my line of vision.)

There's a struggle in the corridor and, while Beach screams for help. Arkin watches helplessly until all three sweating, frantic men dart back into the room and the door slams in his face. Rich asks the cast to do it a second time. His face is ecstatic as he explains, "That's a print!"

Into Room 380, Carol dutifully returns, taking the same position on the rumpled bed and resuming our interview. One leg in a nylon swings back into the air and again the spiked heel seems intent on murder and mayhem. Again she's warm and friendly, reminiscent of the informal way she often spoke directly to her TV audiences during on-air question-and-answer sessions.

"I've never had a master plan regarding my career," she tells me, when asked if there are unfulfilled goals as an actress. "I've always taken things as they come. My husband [producer Joseph Hamilton] likes to kid me. He says if I don't work for twenty straight minutes I think I'm out of the business. But I want you to know: I have no intention of retiring. On the other hand, my life no longer depends on my work. If I don't want a script, I'll easily refuse it.

Carol Burnett during her golden years on CBS television.

"Do you know what I really want to do? I want to grow up to be Ruth Gordon or Hermione Gingold. I want to be an interesting great grandmother. I want to be an active, active old, old lady."

Chu Chu and the Philly Flash is the latest in only a handful of films Carol Burnett has appeared in since 1963, when she made her screen debut in *Who's Been Sleeping in My Bed?* opposite Dean Martin. She hated that one, calling it "a throwaway comedy." She didn't think much of the next one, *Pete 'n Tillie*, made in 1972 with Walter Matthau. Next came her whacky prostitute in Billy Wilder's *Front Page,* a colorful update of the old newspaper comedy that deserved better than the box office rejection it received. Still, she hated the way she had screamed her lines and preferred not to see it or think about it ever again.

Carol slid into a different kind of screen persona in Robert Altman's *A Wedding,* playing the mother of the bride, a Southerner named Tulip, who falls for the uncle of the bridegroom. To Carol, the film was "my best work if not my best part," and it was a "pure and delightful" experience working with a director who encouraged improvisational bits from his cast. "I'm not particularly good at improvising," she confesses, "but Altman gives you a sense of freedom. He wants you to suggest and try things. I always feel in character working with him." The working relationship was so good that Altman invited her back in the summer of 1979 to make *Health,* a film now playing in Los Angeles that depicts a convention of health-food enthusiasts. "Nuts" might be a better description. "I play a political idealist once married to James Garner, who is a sleazy press agent. I think it's the most commercial picture Altman has directed yet, but ever since the lousy reaction to *Quartet,* Fox has been leery of Bob, and I have a fear they might not release the film in other parts of the country." Carol has also made a film with Alan Alda, the comedy *The Four Seasons*.

Television is not a dead issue with her, not by a long shot. She has two variety specials in the planning stages—one with Dudley Moore as narrator/pianist/singer. The other is an ABC special from a Broadway theater featuring Julie Andrews and Beverly Sills.

Carol is interrupted one final time by director Rich, who asks her to return to the corridor. Outside Room 380. She positions herself, her spiked heels digging into the carpet. Despite the din around her, she looks relaxed and poised, staring up at the overhead lights with meditative curiosity. For just a moment, Carol is the only calm in a storm of cinematic confusion.

Sorry to report that Carol's daughter, Carrie, died at the age of thirty-eight of lung and brain cancer. Carol came back with her own show in 1990, *Carol & Company*, which lasted for just a season and a half. She has always stayed busy with television, appearing in the soap opera parody, *Fresno*, and countless other programs.

JAMES COCO
Munching and Lunching
With Boiling Hot Coco
Who Melts Into One Rude Dude

James Coco looks like the happiest man in the world. He sits in the restaurant at the Campton Place Hotel, radiating a warm welcome, apparently luxuriating in euphoria about the fact he is now a lightweight 190 pounds after spending too many years weighing 300 or more. Much more.

Before our interview is over on this day in February 1985, he will demonstrate a less pleasant side to his personality. There will also be nothing happy or funny in sight. For the moment, he is all smiles, the happy-go-lucky James Coco of stage, movies, and TV, and now the author of a best-selling book, the very thing that has brought us together.

People who lose a massive amount of weight sometimes look gaunt and unhealthy, but not Coco. He is the essence of a court jester, radiant and witty, instantly making himself accessible. One of his trademarks, the bald head, hasn't changed, and he looks across the table at me through gold-rimmed glasses with twinkling interest. His own curiosity, in fact, leads him to ask questions about his interviewer; if ever a reporter could feel at ease, it is in his company. "Please call me Jimmy," he says. (Well, at ease for the moment, anyway.)

Wearing a dark brown suit with his Brooks Brothers tie slightly loosened at the throat, Jimmy even looks better in person than he does on the cover of the newly issued Bantam paperback edition of his *The James Coco Diet*, co-written with Marion Paone. The hardcover version came out about a year ago and sold very well. I have read this new version, and found it unusual, for it turned out to be more than a series of recipes.

The James Coco Diet also stirred me in a different way, for Jimmy had dealt with his personal problems of carrying an over-

This is the cover of James Coco's book about his years of trying to lose weight. It was the reason we met, but I would lose my appetite for it, and him, after our luncheon was over.

weight body for most of his life. Roly poly had led not to just body weight disorders but psychological disorders—mental issues that had affected his personal life—such as those moments when he would explode with anger while with family members and friends. Something about how all that ingested food caused an imbalance in his personal behavior. Fascinating, and so honest.

While the writing is light-hearted and breezy, he confesses to an obsession with food and amphetamines—"uppers by day, downers by night"—all designed to lose weight. He admits to fluctuating between high and low moods, "going through Jekyll-and-Hyde personal swings." Affectionate one moment, raging mad the next.

In 1974, at the suggestion of fellow comedian Buddy Hackett, Jimmy began the first of several visits to the Structure House in Durham, N.C., which he says taught him how to come to grips with the psychological problems causing his obesity. As a result of frequent returns to Structure House, he managed to lose more than 100 pounds and thus embarked on a new chapter in his life and career. Show business now had a new, relatively slender figure.

In the book, he stresses that obesity is a behavioral problem, with psychological causes. "There's not a fat person in the world who doesn't know that to be true," Jimmy tells me. "Dealing with it is something else. People have to be overwhelmingly motivated about their conditions to help themselves." Losing weight "breaks down into three parts: a third of it for yourself, a third for your relationships with others, and a third for your work or profession."

Jimmy talks about how he stopped lying to himself to overcome his periods of "fat man misery" and the times he "flew wildly off the handle."

Jimmy was born and raised in New York City, son of a shoemaker. Even in his teen years he was fascinated with acting, but by the time he was in his mid-twenties, he was overweight and prematurely bald. Nevertheless, he was able to land some good character roles on Broadway and off-Broadway. Gradually, he learned the importance of nutrition. "I grew up, I stopped the gimmick diets, and I dealt with food on a real, personal basis. Now I'm in a place where I can have a pizza or ice cream if I want it. I'm not in the same head as I was back in those early days. I know I can stop myself or control my wild urges."

Jimmy leaves the table for a short while. When he comes back, my blood almost freezes when he casually tells me that he has a penchant for watching "whole boxes" of commercial and pornographic movies when he isn't busy making a movie or TV show. Pornography is not a subject I had spruced up on for our conversation.

"You look good," he says to me. "You don't have any weight problems. Stay as you are." He asks me my weight but I'm not sure and tell him that. "What? You don't know your own weight? A fat person always knows his weight to the ounce. Believe me, don't worry. Looking at you, I can tell. You can eat whatever you want."

He goes back to discussing the new Jimmy. "Now," he says, "I see things I never saw before when I take a shower or glance into a mirror. I buy my clothes off a rack instead of going to a fat man's shop and having a size 54 suit custom made. I'm sexually active day and night." He laughs, as if he is just kidding me. "And now I can keep the lights on all night long." He bursts out laughing again.

Jimmy muses about portraying Willy the Plumber in Drano TV commercials, of playing in such Broadway hits as *Auntie Mame*, *Bell, Book and Candle*, and *A Shot in the Dark*. One of his favorites was written just for him by playwright Neil Simon, *Last of the Red Hot Lovers*, for which Jimmy received a Tony Award nomination. Among his favorite movies are *Man of La Mancha* (as Sancho Panza), *Murder By Death*, and *The Cheap Detective*.

"Sometimes," he tells me, "I think about the parts I didn't get because of my weight. Now I'm getting different kinds of roles." He describes his dual characterizations in "Marionettes Inc.," an episode of HBO's *Ray Bradbury Theater*. He has also done a comedy hour for TV, *Day to Day Affair*, a collection of classic revue sketches in which he plays several different parts opposite Jessica Walter, Jack Gilford, and Joyce Van Patten.

The salad and main courses arrive. Jimmy picks up his grilled scallops as he talks about some of his more recent movies, such as *The Muppets Take Manhattan* and the Italian film, *Swiss Cheese*. In the latter, he played a Roman prince, but "something was lost in the translation." Then, the talk switches to a film made in 1981, *Only When I Laugh*, for which he was nominated for an Oscar. "You've seen it, of course."

I shake my head no, and suddenly, Jimmy's mood changes instantly as if a hand grenade has exploded, smoke and shrapnel are filling the dining room, and he has gone into attack mode. "What?" he says, his body stiffening. "You didn't see *Only When I Laugh*? How dare you!" He pushes his luncheon plate away, obvi-

This was the James Coco I remember when our interview began, well-dressed, well-mannered, witty.

ously angry that this alleged reporter doesn't know more about this vitally important film.

I decide to change the subject as quickly as I can and ask him to describe what it takes to be a comedy actor in so many different media. His irritation intensifies and he glares across the table at me. "Comedy actor? No, I'm not a comedy actor. I'm a *serious* actor. I've played a variety of roles and I've won or been nominated for many acting awards. I think of myself as an actor, period!"

By now, he is grimacing at me. The anger in his voice climbs in pitch. His smile has completely vanished. He accuses me of asking stupid questions!

He accuses me of coming to this interview with "a list of slanted questions," with preconceived conclusions designed to trick him, to lead him into a journalistic trap. This whole thing, he screams at me, has been a sham designed to humiliate him in print.

I make an effort to calm him down, and it seems to work, for his mood instantly changes. In a calm voice, he returns to the subject of acting, explaining that "truthful reaction" is what acting is all about. Then, he suddenly turns angry again. In a snarling voice he accuses me again of "stupid questions," of diabolically plotting an ambush. In a screaming voice, accuses me of not having read his book.

That is the irony of the moment. I have read the book, and in that book he had described the very problem he was now demonstrating to me at the top of his voice, his inability to control his emotions should a negative thought invade his sanity. Next, he points a finger at me like a weapon. "I'm going to interview Rex Reed and John Simon, and all of the movie critics who're always interviewing *us*. And I'm gonna do *my* interview with you and I'm gonna have it printed in *The New York Times*."

Jimmy throws down his napkin and storms away from the table. He pauses at the maitre'd check-in stand, shouting at the top of his voice. This time, his audience is everyone in the dining room.

Finally, he steps out into Campton Alley, where it is sunny but chilly. A limousine is parked at the curb, awaiting his return. I step into the alley behind him. He sees me and shakes his head, rushing to get into the limo as if he wants to escape the situation as quickly as possible. "This is terrible," he remarks as he opens the rear door. Then, he slides into the back seat.

As I take a few steps closer to the limo, he shakes his finger at me and at the top of his voice screams, "Remember, I'm writing a story about you! In *The New York Times*!" The rear window comes down and he leans toward me, his head coming through the window. "You'll be reading it!"

The limo pulls away from the curb, and I hear one more cry, "You'll be reading it!"

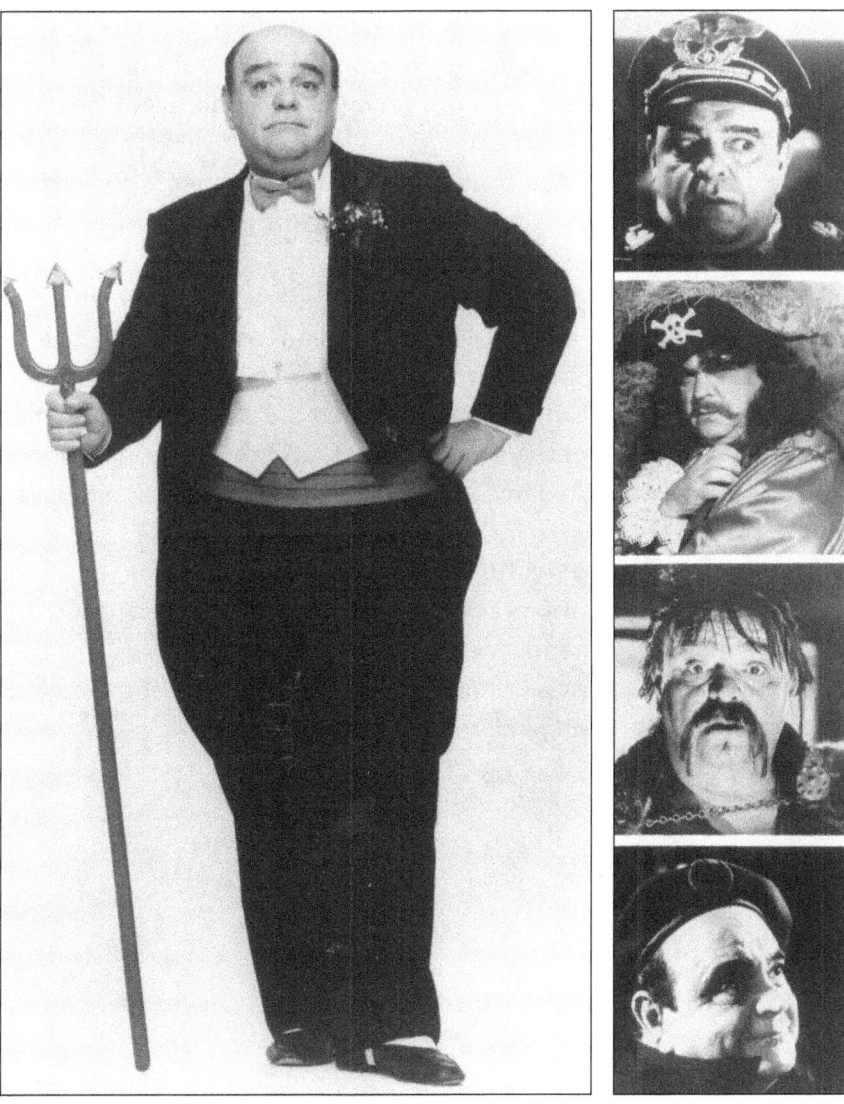

This is James Coco in his last major film, Hunk, *portraying Dr. D. At right are four of the disguises he wears in his portrayal of The Devil.*

Naturally, Jimmy's publicity agent comes to see my editor, David Kleinberg, to complain about how I had upset the cookbook author during our meal. When I was confronted by Kleinberg, I read him the following paragraph from the book, which dealt with a period in his life when he was hooked on amphetamines, or diet pills:

"I was going through Jekyll-and-Hyde personality swings . . . even my closest friends who have never failed me stopped calling.

I was too much to handle. I must have been a monster during that period. The personality change was so schizoid none of my friends wanted to deal with me anymore. My behavior became too bizarre and unpredictable."

David and I concluded that Jimmy must have been hooked on those pills again, for his self-description was exactly how he had behaved that afternoon.

James Coco had just two years left to live, almost to the day of our meeting. He died in 1987 of a heart attack at the age of fifty-six. Ironically, there is an episode of *The Jeffersons* entitled "Treehouse of Horror IV" (1993) in which a demon forces Homer Simpson to eat donuts as a punishment, and the demon remarks, "I don't understand it. James Coco went mad in fifteen minutes." In my case, it took him a little longer to flip out.

The very year he died, he appeared in the film, *Hunk*, in which he portrayed Dr. D, who is actually the Devil. He agrees to turn an average man into a handsome, woman-chasing stud.

Although I was sent a publicity photo, I never saw the film, and I still haven't seen *Only When I Laugh*.

ADRIENNE BARBEAU
The Beautiful Brunette
Who Scrubbed Off 'Grease'
And Came to Maude's House

Late in 1972, Adrienne Barbeau, a beautiful brunette, sits in the semi darkness of the Record Room, the cocktail lounge at the Hollywood Brown Derby, a popular gathering point for makers of movies and TV show. Despite the low-key lighting, there is a high-key

Adrienne Barbeau autographed this publicity photo to my daughter Trista.

charm and poise to the twenty-seven-year-old woman perched on a barstool, and there is a self-assurance that is unmistakable.

Adrienne Barbeau begins by telling me a story about how she once sat alone in the ladies' room of a New Jersey dive, reading a book on how to become an actress. She wanted desperately to be a performer at that moment, but the necessity of eating, and being free during the daytime to try out for auditions, had forced her to take whatever night job she could grab.

That job had turned out to be that of a discotheque dancer. Most of the other young women that gyrated and did the grind in glass cages or atop the liquor-stained bar were pure hookers, but Adrienne had a reputation in the joint for being a non-hooker. More than one ogling dude had absorbed her slaps, and she had a cool way of ignoring the most suggestive comments from the male clientele.

Between acts, Adrienne sat in the joint, read, and dreamed about a day when maybe, just maybe, she would grow into a legitimate actress. Not a grinder of those parts that tend to attract male attention.

That's the scene Adrienne paints when she talks about her initiation to the New York syndrome known as "the acting world." I just kept telling myself," she goes on, "that I was going to make it one day . . . I was going to make it . . . and finally the jobs weren't so crummy anymore and I was doing stock and plays and I was actually earning a decent living as an actress. God, I couldn't believe it. I was making it."

While the prospects of fame and fortune crumble for some who might work as hard as Adrienne (and who might dream just as vividly), they solidified on the Great White Way of Broadway, first as one of the daughters in *Fiddler on the Roof*, then as a wiggly young thing in *Grease*, a rock musical that won her a Tony nomination and a Theater World Award as Most Promising Actress.

She was cast in the role of Carol, the daughter of *Maude* (Beatrice Arthur) on the popular sitcom Maude, the real reason I was meeting Adrienne that afternoon. She had been divorced at the age of twenty-seven with an eight-year-old son in tow, and hence needed somewhere to live as the series began.

Adrienne Barbeau as Carol with Bea Arthur (mother Maude) in an episode of their successful CBS series.

Adrienne was still in *Grease* when producer Norman Lear (and the man who created *Maude*) tracked her down. "There was this call from CBS," she recalls, "and I thought, *Oh brother, here we go. Soap opera work five days a week. Oh, brother.* Then, it became clear that they were considering me for the role of Maude's daughter, which had first been played by Marsha Rodd in a spin-off episode that had been shown on *All in the Family* earlier in the year.

Adrienne Barbeau with filmmaker John Carpenter, whom she married on January 1, 1979. They would have a son, John Cody, and would also come together to create his sci-fi and horror films of the early 1980s

"Marsha, it turned out, didn't want to leave her family and move to the West Coast. But I, well, I was willing. But then they thought I was too young and I went back to *Grease* and stewed for a while and then, in two weeks, they called me back.

"My God, there I was in Hollywood again, this time being asked to put down this poor dressed boy, and so I did, without being too nasty. I guess they were impressed because they were smiling a lot. Back to New York I went, and damn, they called me again, and I thought, *Here we go again, another audition*. But this time, they

Adrienne Barbeau, after establishing herself as a comedienne on Maude, *became a sex symbol in the late 1970s, offering up a cheesecake calendar.*

wanted me. Really wanted me. Can you imagine that? Out of all those girls, they wanted me. The whole thing was unreal."

As all her emotion pours out uninhibitedly, Adrienne claims she built up her sense of self-assuredness by living in New York for so many years, where "just trying to register a complaint with the phone company could lead to a traumatic withdrawal from society. The folks back east are pretty uptight, and you get tough along with the rest of them, just to survive."

So this brunette seated next to me is tough in spirit, but not in looks. She has all the soft places, and today she is wearing a full-length pant suit that is mostly black with a scattering of red roses. The neckline is plunging, and each time she moves, sideways or down, every male head in the room swings with her.

The topic shifts back to TV, and she shrugs at first, uncertain of what to say. The series *Maude* ... well, it's so new ... she doesn't want to say anything that might ... oh well ... she throws her head, moistens her lips, and plunges ahead.

"I'm still adjusting to the transition to TV. I feel a certain amount of frustration because after the stage I'm used to lots of preparation time and TV doesn't offer that luxury. Carol? Oh, she's a pretty straight girl. She's strong, trying to make it in a man's world. I guess you could almost say I'm playing myself, except I'm the kind that would never live at home again."

That home she won't be going back to is in San Jose, CA, where she was raised and educated at Del Mar High School. Her mother had encouraged her toward music and dancing at an early age, and she participated in high school and community theater. When the San Jose Light Opera received a federal grant to tour the Pacific, she went along and entertained American troops in Southeast Asia, a cutting of the umbilical cord.

In New York, she began to study drama under Warren Roberts at the same time she began the grueling experience of auditions by day, menial, oft-depressing jobs by night.

Adrienne admits she doesn't particularly like comedy, especially TV comedy. "Most of it is ridiculous because you can't relate to anything in it. It has no social satire. At least *Maude* is different in that it deals with attitudes and problems of today, and tries to give you something that could make you think. Mom [Maude] is always trying to please the maid, Florida, by avoiding any reminder she's Black.

"I've been doing a lot of thinking about all my friends back in New York, the ones eking out an existence, struggling to reach the top. I hope they don't give up. I hope they keep working because if they believe in something strongly enough, hey, they can make it come true"

Adrienne Barbeau will continue co-starring in *Maude* for all of its run, appearing in ninety-seven episodes as the beautiful Carol

Traynor, and building a reputation as a sex symbol. She continues to build that sexy profile with a calendar of so-called "cheesecake" shots in 1978. Then, her career takes a "horror-ible" turn away from comedy. In 1979, she marries horror film director John Carpenter, and her career for the next few years will now move into the arena of horror.

My second meeting with the personable Adrienne Barbeau takes place in October 1985, a little more than a year after she has divorced John Carpenter. A white limousine pulls into the driveway of the Hotel Meridien, where I am waiting. The chauffeur pops out to open the back door, and a pair of shapely limbs in yellow high heels slides into my view. The woman who follows, lovely and stately in a yellow knit sweater (though with conservative neckline), is Adrienne, as beautiful as when I met her back in 1972. Seated in the back of the limo is a nanny taking care of her seventeen-month-old son, John Cody Carpenter. She gives the child a wave goodbye as the limo pulls away and we go inside for lunch.

As we are seated, I cannot help but admire the fact that she is wearing a minimum of makeup, yet stands out like no other woman in the room. "Thank you for seeing me," she begins. "I love being back in action. I love taking care of my son and he'll always come first, but I also need adult interaction, the exchange of ideas with other people like you."

She tells me she first met Carpenter while portraying a "lesbian victim" in the TV movie *High Rise* (aka *Someone Is Watching*) and married him, leaving the TV field behind to star in many of his films. "I had quite a time making sci-fi and horror films. It started with the tough, gritty Maggie in John's *Escape From New York*, and then as the terrorized disc jockey in John's *The Fog*. Then, there was the resilient scientist I played in Wes Craven's *Swamp Thing*."

Next up, she says, will be an episode of *The Twilight Zone* called "Gargoyle," which she describes as a tour de force for any actress. "This is a portrait of a woman turning into a monster but with the woman always underneath the ugly physiognomy, struggling to stop the monster from happening. I've never turned into a monster before, but I found the experience exhilarating . . . it's

Adrienne Barbeau caught up in a cycle of horror as Wilma in the episode "The Crate" from George A. Romero's 1984 Stephen King anthology film, Creepshow.

fun to create something new, even if I don't hang out with a lot of gargoyles. It's difficult to know how big or small to be when you project."

When lunch is finished, we hurry back to the hotel entrance, where Adrienne's limo is waiting. Young John Cody rushes into her arms as she slides into the back seat. She waves excitedly one last time as the car pulls away into downtown traffic.

I was able to contact Adrienne Barbeau in the summer of 2015 while preparing this book. I asked her to describe the effect *Maude* had on her career. "It was immeasurable. For so many reasons, in addition to the obvious one of introducing me to a national TV viewing audience.

"I learned comedy timing from Bea Arthur, one of the greatest comediennes of the era—of any era. I met my first comedy writing genius: Norman Lear. Made loving friends who stayed loving friends throughout our lives. Conrad Bain? I miss him every day. And because the media looked to me as a spokesperson for the women's issues we dealt with on the show, I quickly developed an understanding of my beliefs about those issues. Up until *Maude*, I was a young woman hoping to earn a living at what she loved; not thinking about much else except how to accomplish that, and, of course, any romance that might come my way. *Maude* pushed me to consider so very much more. And it was the basis for everything in my career that followed.

"I have written an autobiography, *There Are Worse Things I Can Do*. As for my acting roles . . . *Carnivale* [2003-2005] was one of my all time favorite jobs, and Ruthie one of my favorite roles. Everything about it, from the cast to the writers, the crew to the producers, the network, the location, even the caterers! I believe it gave rise to so many successful series that followed, and it was canceled way too soon. One more season and the numbers would have surpassed what the network was hoping for. We were just a little before our time."

CONRAD BAIN
How Conrad Got Hooked on Shelter Island
–All in a Comedy Bain

Because Adrienne Barbeau was so emotional about her feelings for Conrad Bain, her co-star on *Maude*, I decided to include him in this book, based on an interview from 1975.

Off the coast of New York, not far in terms of travel but very far in terms of escaping the jungle of Manhattan, there are twelve square miles of lightly populated land known as Shelter Island.

Conrad has been slowly building his own dream home there for the past few years because he found Shelter Island "a marvelous place to hibernate" when he isn't working on Broadway or in motion pictures. When he portrayed Dr. Arthur Harmon, the neighbor on *Maude*, he came to realize his home wasn't as isolated as he imagined.

One of the pleasures of living on Shelter is the fishing—striped bass, bluefish, and bottom fish are plentiful. One day recently, Conrad took to his rowboat and dropped his fishing line, only to become hopelessly entangled in a gill net cast earlier by a pair of fishermen. As Conrad fought to free the propeller of his outboard motor, two fellows in yellow slickers rowed by. "Hey," shouted one in a Brooklyn accent, "it's the guy from *Maude*!" The other guy blurted, "Wait'll I tell Ma. She won't believe it when she hears we caught a celebrity!"

"At first," recalls Conrad, as he recounts to me his narrative, "I thought you could get away and have no ties to the rest of the real world. I realized at that moment such a belief is impossible, anywhere on this globe floating through space. But I still love being out there and communing with nature, even if I do have a hook in my back, figuratively speaking. And fishing, of course. My wife, Monica, loves to garden and plant, and one of these days I'm really going to pursue my hobby, sculpturing. If I could just stop from going off in so many directions at once...."

Conrad Bain

Those directions include TV, motion pictures, and theater, Off-Broadway and on Broadway. Conrad, at the age of fifty-two, finds all these outlets for acting "enormously exciting in terms of exploring characterizations. I always take a deep, long look at the men I play, searching for the things hidden beneath their surfaces."

In TV, however, Conrad will no doubt remain for some time to come, for *Maude* (now in its second season) has lost none of its popularity in the ratings, remaining one of the most watched of the current batch of Norman Lear situation comedies filling the airwaves.

"When Lear conceived this show," explains Conrad, "he wanted a woman liberal with a capital L. To infuse conflict into the situation, he needed an opposite—a conservative neighbor. He discarded the idea of an accountant, and settled instead for a doctor. And that became me. Or Doc Harmon. But now, even some of those original concepts have undergone gradual alterations. Maude, for example, is more vulnerable and less unrelenting than earlier. And my relationship with her has changed. At first it was simply abrasive. Then Lear insisted there must be some indication of affection, for beneath all disagreement there is positive human connection, or love.

"It's funny, but the characters take on a life of their own after a while that have nothing to do with Beatrice Arthur [Maude] or Conrad Bain. Every script explores some new concept of the mind, giving us, as actors, the chance to open up our range of abilities."

Conrad came to acting after a difficult period in Alberta, Canada, his birthplace. There, he often worked on farms to pay his way through the Banff School of Fine Arts. His own attempt as a farm owner ended in failure, but he had little time to worry about that. He was soon a sergeant in the Canadian Army and remained so for all of World War II.

After graduating from the American Academy of Dramatic Arts in 1948, with fellow classmate Don Rickles not far from his side, Conrad then endured ten years of stock company productions before his Broadway debut in 1956 in *The Iceman Cometh*. Credits in films, TV (two seasons in *Dark Shadows* as innkeeper Wells), and theater have been lengthy ever since.

Conrad is casual in dress and easy-going in manner, suggesting he is following no master plan. He admits as much. "I've never been ambitious in the conventional sense. All you can say is that I work a lot, and I intend to keep on working. If some greater success evolves out of that, fine. If not, I'll be satisfied to work wherever I'm wanted."

As for Shelter Island, that still fits into his master plan. "Just say I'm hooked. In June, the bluefish run like you wouldn't believe. And you better believe that I'll be there. If I have some good lines on *Maude*, you can bet I'll have some good lines plopped straight down into the water."

Conrad stuck with *Maude* for 118 of its 141 episodes, moving on to play Philip Drummond in 189 episodes of *Diff'rent Strokes* (1978-86) and Charlie Ross in 24 episodes of *Mr. President* (1987-88). He and his wife, Monica, would enjoy "Bain's Island" (Shelter Island) on and off through the years until she died in 2009. He died just short of his ninetieth birthday in Livermore, CA, in 2013.

SALLY STRUTHERS
A Lousy Day on the Bio-Curve For Sally Struthers–But Hey, It's All in Her TV Family

I cannot remember meeting an actress as wound up as Sally Struthers on a day in December 1972, when we meet for lunch. It isn't to be much of a lunch for her, as she only smokes cigarettes to satisfy her appetite.

If we are to believe a Beverly Hills researcher named Mike Wallerstein, who is constantly feeding mountains of material into the handiest computer, we all have something called Bio-Curve. No, not the kind of curve that is given three numbers, as in 35-26-38, or the shape that captures your eye at a Burlesque show or topless club.

Rather, Bio-Curve is based on the idea we're designed like clocks; that from birth to death, we undergo a series of physical, emotional, and mental cycles, cycles that are ever-changing, ever on the upswing, ever on the downswing. Thus, Waterloo was a zero-point on Napoleon's Bio-Curve. As for General George Armstrong Custer, the curve goes right off the scale for June 25, 1876.

The folks at the CBS Television City Commissary are busily discussing Mr. Wallenstein's theory as it relates to the upcoming Super Bowl clash between the Redskins and the Dolphins. It only seems a natural extension of things, therefore, to relate the idea of Bio-Curve to Sally Struthers as she comes hurrying toward the table for a luncheon interview. She is moving fast, she is very bouncy, and her attire gives every indication she is a woman in love with life, who possibly doesn't have an inhibition in the book.

The eyes goes immediately to the bright red knee socks that bump somewhere just below her knees, against a pair of tight-fitting blue jeans, and which appear they are about to pop at any second. Above the tight blue jeans, when the movement shifts the material just right, is a portion of bare midriff. Then comes a

Despite her dislike of giving autographs, Sally Struthers gladly signed this photo to me with "Thanks for putting up with a 'low.' And Happy New Year!"

pink sweater—baby pink—and very sensuous, a definite enhancement to her light complexion and flowing blonde hair. A little eyebrow shadow is in evidence, but otherwise no obvious signs of make-up. Not even lipstick. This is a girl, one decides, who puts her trust in her natural assets.

The Bio-Curve, in her case, would surely register high. After all, this is a moment in the career of Sally Struthers when she is known world-wide for her role as Gloria Stivic, daughter of racist daddy Archie Bunker (Carroll O'Connor) on *All in the Family*. A young woman living through the kind of career upswing a thousand other working actresses would give anything to experience.

Sorry, Wallerstein, but outward appearances must not have much to do with Bio-Curve. Sally is on a downer from the moment she plunks into a chair and informs everybody she has no intentions of eating and that she can't stay too long because she has a dress-fitting session, and anyway, she can't understand why anyone, from a newspaper or not, would want to talk to her. She's a big drag dullsville type. The only pause during all this is when she lights up a Marlboro, after which she begins describing all the things that have been wrong these past few days.

"Oh, I'm tired. I'm exhausted. Flu. I've just got over the flu. My body fought off every bug in the book. I had bronchitis. It was terrible. I keep dozing off during the rehearsals. I'm feeling old today. I'm like an old lady. I want to get back to my normal energy level. I need that energy to survive being an actress. You need undying energy in this crazy business."

No way to get that Bio-Curve up, even when the conversation shifts to *All in the Family*. "At this stage," says Sally, lighting up another Marlboro, "the fun has gone out of playing Gloria. Gloria's the least interesting of all the show's characters. She has the least to do. As a rule, I have so few lines. 'Let me help you set the table, Mom.' 'Daddy, why do you talk that way?' 'Mike, let's go to bed, I'm tired.' These things I can learn by sheer repetition during rehearsals. I never have to look at the scripts. It's so stifling, confining. I'm a girl who loves to express my feelings. I love to scream, to cry, all those emotional things. Gloria is so unfulfilling. I have to keep reacting without saying anything. Archie and Edith [that would be mother, played by Jean Stapleton] are the caricatures, as everything is written for them. And for that husband of mine, Mike!" (That would be Rob Reiner *before* he became a movie director.)

Yes, she has suggested building the character of Gloria to the producers, but fat chance! "I'm worried sick about being typecast the rest of my life. The very thought of playing Gloria, or girls like her, to the end of my days is a recurring nightmare. Here I worked and worked to get the door open, and now it's swinging shut on me and somehow I've got to find a way to keep my foot wedged against it, to keep it ajar."

Sally wants people to look upon her as a dramatic actress and as a singer-dancer. "That's how I got my start, doing variety specials with Herb Alpert, the Smothers Brothers, Tim Conway. This last summer, I went away on my hiatus to play the part of this sexy girl in San Peckinpah's *The Getaway*. A mindless bimbo, an aging overripe nymph, that's what some of the critics called her. It was the total opposite of Gloria, I can tell you that much. I'm this veterinarian's wife who decides to shack up with another guy. Now maybe they'll stop looking at me as a girl and see me as I want to be seen–as a woman." (During the sexy scenes, they certainly were watching.)

The success of *All in the Family* brought Sally instant recognition, which she instantly abhorred. "People feel like they know you personally and they do obnoxious things. They feel like they own you or something. It's reached the point I don't want to go out into public anymore. I want to hide. Be anonymous. I wonder about people who ask for autographs on empty gum wrappers or matchbook covers. It's all so dumb and meaningless."

One of the positive things Sally will be doing when she finishes the current batch of *Family* episodes is to split for Las Vegas, where she'll do a song-and-dance nightclub act.

While it should provide an upward arc on her Bio-Curve, it just might create a plummeting effect. You see, she dislikes Las Vegas. "I don't relish being locked up in the middle of the desert with all those neon lights blazing around me, but it's there I'll have the chance to convince a lot of people I can sing and dance. Right now, my agent tells the producers in this town about my voice and they laugh. All they can see is nice little Gloria Stivic. I'm hitting my head against the wall. Well, after this act, maybe no more. Maybe they'll listen."

Sally pauses to light up her third Marlboro in fifteen minutes. She studies the burning match before shaking it out. "I'm very uncoordinated. My depth perception is bad. Every time I have to swing a tennis racket, or hit a golf ball, I can't quite connect. Like when I'm doing the soft shoe, I can't use a cane. Isn't that maddening? Maybe I should have my eyes checked. Did you know I once injured my knee playing volleyball?"

Obligingly, Sally hikes one of her shapely legs into view, pushing up the leg of her jeans, lowering the bright red sock and exposing a kneecap. A small white scar quells all doubts about her claim. Down goes her leg, up goes the Marlboro. "They say I walk like a truck driver. Sometimes I have to stop and think and try to be lady-like. I can't sit still very long for anything. I've always been hyperactive. You'll have to excuse me in a minute because I have that dress fitting I told you about. And rehearsals . . . all this blasted week!"

She sighs, angling the Marlboro toward her lips again. "I'll be glad when it's over and I can go out and forget about the show for a few days. I never think about the shows when I'm not working. Here, smell this." Sally advances her forearm for me to sniff at. So I sniff sniff sniff. "What you're smelling . . . that's men's cologne. Been using it since Christmas. Everyone's been telling me how good I smell."

Suddenly, without warning, Sally leaps up, stuffing her pack of remaining Marlboros into her purse, which she then slings swiftly over her shoulder. "Almost forgot. My dress fitting. I've got to go. You'll excuse me, please."

Then Sally is on her feet, literally running across the commissary, disappearing out the door in little time. Those eating at surrounding tables—many of them cast members or crew members of *All in the Family*—have paid absolutely no attention to her hasty departure. Whatever Sally Struthers does, and whatever Sally Struthers is, it's all in the family as far as they're concerned.

Sally Struthers is keeping her Bio-Curve much alive in the world of television. For someone who thought playing Gloria was a time-waster, Sally must have been shocked to the core of her soul when she was nominated nine times for an Emmy as Best Supporting Actress. (She would win twice, in 1972 and 1979.) She stayed very busy right after our meeting, appearing in 183 *All in the Family* episodes. She then went on to portray Gloria a few times on *Archie Bunker's Place* in 1979 and 1982 before starring in her own series, *Gloria,* for 21 episodes (1982-83). Her next series, *Nine to Five* (1986-88), gave her 52 episodes. Then, she was the voice of Rebecca Cunningham on *TaleSpin* (1990-91), and the voice of Charlene Sinclair on *Dinosaurs* (2001-2004). She really struck it rich again as Babette Dell on *Gilmore Girls* (2000-2007), completing 52 episodes. Despite the fact she gained a little weight along the way, she's still active as hell. (And I hope she cut back on those Marlboros.)

JEAN STAPLETON
The 'Family' Ding-a-Ling Everybody Wants to Love Is Really a Forever Lady

Edith Bunker is the broadest of caricatures, a funny shuffling housewife with a fatuous voice. She is subservient to a caustic bigot of a husband who seldom shows his love for her; a "ding-a-ling" in the words of that husband, and a naive, cheerful innocent that lacks the ability to realize the lower class deprivations of her own life.

And yet, there are viewers who will tell you that there is something in Jean Stapleton's performance as Edith Bunker that reminds them of women in their own lives, usually a loved one. Perhaps a mother, an aunt, a grandmother, a great-grandmother, or a wife of long-standing.

Therefore, one must assume that *All in the Family* has more of a foundation in the reality of American womanhood than its broad comedy would first indicate. Miss Stapleton, a modest kind of soul to begin with, does not consider herself a psychologist and would rather not get pulled into a deep discussion about what Edith Bunker means in the greater scheme of housewives, or in the milieu of the average middle-aged American mother/wife.

She can only be flattered because to point out these things is to tell her she has captured in her performance some essence of truth. Explicit in that is the flattering presumption that she is really delivering the goods as an actress.

In December 1974, Jean pauses to talk to me during a taping of *All in the Family* at CBS Television City in Hollywood, where, for three seasons, she has helped to attract 66 million Americans on an average Saturday night.

Now, brace yourself for a jolt. To meet Jean is to meet a woman totally alien to all the traits of Edith Bunker, in both appearance and manner. She is wearing a printed pink pants suit that is cut low at the neck and looks very sexy on her, exposing her abun-

Jean Stapleton signed her publicity photo to me and my wife, Erica, when we met at CBS Television City in 1974.

dant bosom abundantly. This and sensuously arranged red hair indicate a preference for glamour over the dowdiness of Mrs. Bunker. She wears little make-up (neither does Edith—credit the transformation to hairstyle, wardrobe and affectation) and she radiates intelligence, charm, warmth. She has a difficult time explaining what it is that is Edith Bunker, deciding that it might be easier if she touched on the character's origin.

"There have been traces of Edith in my other stage and film roles. I've certainly done the nasal thing before, although never to such an extent. A lot of people assume Edith must be patterned after someone close to me, but that's not true. I had a very loveable aunt who had Edith's charm and ability to smile at adversity, but the comparison goes no further. The whole concept behind Edith has to be credited to Norman Lear, one of our producers. He saw the character in his mind's eye and we developed it from there. In a way it's been teamwork which has made *Family* the success it is. The writers hone the scripts; we stand guard to make certain the characters never lose their consistency."

In her own words, Jean feels Edith "is a woman who never gives up hope, who endures situations that often seem hopeless to other housewives. There is never a deep-rooted sense of pain, only hope, love, and the ability to go on and on. She's a forever woman."

While Edith Bunker may go down in TV history as Jean's finest role, and certainly as one of the medium's most memorable creatures, Edith and *All in the Family* remain but one phase of her career. To stop with Edith and grow no further would be tantamount to committing professional suicide. Jean continues to consider her stage work at the Totem Pole Playhouse in Fayetteville, Pennsylvania, vital to her career and peace of mind.

The theater is owned by her husband, William Putch, and it is there she goes during the periods when *All in the Family* is not taping. She calls it "therapy," and "it's the best stimulation in the world for an actress, after playing one role for so long, because it gives you the chance to do a variety of parts. This coming season, for example, we'll be doing two drawing room comedies: *Lullaby* and *Vinegar Free*. Not as many people see you, yet I personally get greater satisfaction knowing I'm a versatile actress again—that I can do many things." She experienced this same satisfaction earlier this year when she appeared in *The Time of the Cuckoo* at the Los Angeles Music Center.

If Miss Stapleton sounds a bit humble, "going home again" for the past seventeen years to do an average of two plays a year, and preferring the grass roots of her profession, she isn't really.

The success of *All in the Family*, and the recognition it has brought her, have definitely gone to her head. "It's expanded my thinking like you wouldn't believe. I'm not seeing the same side of the street. I feel a strong sense of responsibility to my work. From now on I must be very selective about what I do. I must choose with great care."

That's what she says, but those around her say she is still the Jean Stapleton who worked on Broadway (*Damn Yankees, Bells Are Ringing*), the same friendly, good-natured character actress in such films as *Up the Down Staircase, Cold Turkey*, and *Klute*; the same versatile performer who has done TV since the live days of *Studio One, Omnibus*, and *Armstrong Circle Theater*; the same Jean Stapleton of pre-award days before the Emmy, the Genii, and the Golden Globe.

If there is an ego trip involved in her life, she has yet to pack her things and set off on the journey.

Like Sally Struthers, Jean Stapleton stayed with *All in the Family* to the end, winning two Golden Globes and three Emmys as Best Actress. Also like Struthers, she did a handful of appearances on *Archie Bunker's Place*, but then asked to be dropped from the cast. By then, she had utterly tired of the role of Edith Bunker. She would score again in the 1990-1991 series, *Baghdad Café*, as Jasmine Zweibel in fifteen episodes. She continued to appear in plays produced by her husband until his death in 1983. In 2002, she was inducted into the American Theatre Hall of Fame, and one year later was accepted into the Television Hall of Fame. She died at the age of ninety in New York City in 2013.

BARBARA FELDON (*GET SMART*)
An Afternoon With the Tiger Skin Woman: Aka Agent 99 With Siamese Yang

When *Get Smart* premiered on NBC in 1965, it proved to be a successful attempt to satirize the growing popularity of the James Bond movie series, with Agent 007 obviously inspiring the idea to call Maxwell Smart (played by Don Adams) Agent 86. His beautiful lady companion, level-headed and able to "control" 86 when she has to, is only identified as Agent 99 (Barbara Feldon), while the head of the Washington, D.C., agency they spy for, CONTROL, is just plain old "Chief." (In a few early episodes, Ed Platt was identified as Agent Q.) One could not help but think of another inept, bumbling detective by the name of Inspector Clouseau, as the half-hour series unfolds. Also flashing into one's mind in those times were such popular spy thrillers as Britain's *The Avengers* and the U.S. hit show *The Man From U.N.C.L.E.*

The series is the brainchild of comedy writers Mel Brooks and Buck Henry. Brooks will immediately begin writing and directing his own movies (*The Producers* comes first), while Henry goes on to create two TV series, *Captain Nice* and *Quark*.

Get Smart, which will run for a total of 137 episodes for five seasons (1965-1970), is full of running gags. Would you believe . . . ? That is a phrase followed by a ridiculous joke that becomes one of the show's most popular pieces. A telephone hidden away in Maxwell's shoe is another repeated gag. Then, there emerges the Cone of Silence, a huge glass bubble that drops down over Max and the Chief whenever they begin conversations about secret doings, after which Max can't hear a word the Chief is saying.

So allow me to ask . . . would you believe that I have the good fortune to interview all three principals during the time when the show is highly rated on Saturday nights? It begins in the summer of 1966 during one of my trips to Hollywood.

Just off Sunset Boulevard, on the eastern fringe of the Hollywood Strip, stands stately Chateau Marmont, a seven-story hotel

Barbara Feldon, aka Agent 99 or Tiger Skin.

that, since the early days of filmdom, has catered almost exclusively to stars in search of solitude from their overwhelming moments of fame.

Its celebrated residents are usually long-staying, in some cases permanent, and because of well-enforced security measures they are seldom bothered by outsiders.

Unfortunately for Barbara Feldon, the adept Agent 99 and partner of the inept Agent 86 on *Get Smart*, there is no way she can deny me when I arrive for an interview in the summer of 1966, imposed upon her by NBC's publicity department. On the other hand, at no time will she address me as Agent Number One.

Room 5-A turns out to be an ornately-decorated though not overly-large apartment in which the tall, slender actress is at work on her latest painting. Scattered across the room are at least fifteen of her oil canvases, most of them abstract and colorful, and admittedly created for her own "psychoanalysis."

On this afternoon of domestic leisure for Barbara, she is barefooted, dressed in a simple print shift, and made up only with a pale lipstick. Winding its tail around her ankle is her Siamese friend, Yang Pussy Cat.

"Would you believe it?" she asks me, rubbing that shapely ankle against Yang. "There isn't a single 'Tiger Skin' in the entire place." This is an allusion to her past TV career as the Top Brass hair cream girl curled up on a tiger-skin rug, going "Ggggrrrrr, all you men." That was preceded by her girl-in-the-towel-wearing-nothing-else as she sold deodorant pads with a five-day life span. "It all belongs to the past," she says, leaning toward me to end her sentence with "Ggggrrrrr."

Taking a chair by an open balcony that looks partially out over a bleak sprawl of Los Angeles suburbia, and partially onto a steep, deeply green hillside bathed in smog-free sunlight, Barbara begins peeling apples, which will serve as her lunch.

I don't bother to ask if I can have the leftover core. I just sit beside her, enjoying the outdoor air. "I love to sit in this same spot in the mornings," she tells me. "You should see the view at 6 a.m., just before I leave for the studio. I have to sound like a Pollyanna, but I don't mind a bit getting up so early. There are the last vestiges of night—a sliver of moon and stars. Everything has a Mediterranean look at that hour, as you often see in the south of France. The sun creaks over the hilltop and a yellowish-pink glow reflects off the surrounding buildings."

Barbara is a fashionable young woman who makes her home in New York when she isn't filming episodes of *Get Smart*. She is extremely candid, to the point of admitting she has a "Voguish straight-up-and-down figure."

Finished with the apples, she pats Yang on the head. Yang is always beside her, purring and hoping for a scratch or tickle on the head. "Both my husband, Lucien [Verdoux-Feldon], who is a professional photographer, and I are pushovers for animals. Yang is an incredible cat, has a musical way of talking. Listen."

I listen. The sleek feline responds as if she understands English and very quickly gets that tickle on the head from the Master. "Yang is like a child in many ways. So spoiled. Back in our New York apartment, we have a Puli dog named Sacha. A lumbering playmate. It's really like a menagerie when we're all together."

Barbara flushes with excitement when I ask her about her co-starring role opposite Don Adams, and the fact that the second season will be starting soon. "Agent 99, there's a woman. She has such a different psychology from the 'Tiger Girl,' which was a soft sell—a spoof. Now 99 is not a siren, nor is she tongue-in-cheek. She's a straightforward, sweet career woman trying to do her job as devotedly as possible." The real humor of *Get Smart*, she adds, is the incongruous. "As 99, I'm worth two Agent 49s any day. I have to look out not only for myself but Max, as well. It's almost a maternal caring. I'm currently getting him out of his predicaments with some feminine ingenuity (like a hair pin or ring), or giving him advice because I know he can't handle the situation by himself.

"I'll say 'Max, why don't you look in the closet for the body, then call the Chief.' Indignantly, Max'll reply, 'Please, 99, I'd rather do this myself. Now let's see. I think I'll look in the closet for the body and then call the Chief.'"

Get Smart was last season's big cluck-and-gag hit, as all the "Would you believe it?" jokes would indicate (there is even an edition of these jokes currently in book form.) Barbara also points out other running gags that have become household phrases: "Sorry about that, Chief"; "And loving it" (preceded by a warning to Smart that he will soon be subjected to grave dangers).

Has there been any conflict of image between 99 and 'Tiger Girl?'

"None whatsoever," she replies flatly. "They're really two non-conflicting interests, and I respect both. Oh, I have run into condescension over commercial appearances, but that's so fallacious.

It's every bit as creative as a character role, since you are trying to sell a product.

"Most people in the business will tell you that doing a commercial means the end of the line. For me, however, it was just the beginning. It came at a fortunate time, so that I was able to develop in other areas, such as acting."

The "Tiger Girl" exposure led to a handful of TV parts (including George C. Scott's girlfriend on the series *East Side, West Side*, and two episodes of *Flipper*) and finally to the stylishly-dressed Agent 99.

"I took the role as a risk, because I had always vowed never to live in Los Angeles. Without New York, I'm like a baby without a bottle. I'm glad, though, I took that risk because—believe it or not—I've grown to like this community. It does have its good sides, after all."

Barbara has seemingly always aspired toward acting. She was brought up in Pittsburgh under the name Barbara Anne Hall, and eventually attended Carnegie Tech drama school. "Then, I went to New York to become an actress. What other goal in life could there be for somebody as starry-eyed as I was? But, after a go at it, I decided Broadway could do nicely without me. (Or was it the other way around?) I just didn't have the fortitude and patience it demands."

Which is why Barbara went into modeling. Someone suggested TV commercial work, but an authority in the field told her that limpid eyes and a sultry mouth such as hers never sold anything. (This was, she points out, just before the Soft Sell became the vogue.) She still permits an agency to arrange assignments at a commercial studio.

"I was in tears," says Barbara with that sultry mouth, batting her limpid eyeballs. "They wouldn't even turn the cameras on me. But, I was wishy-washy enough at that time to be pushed around by others, and wound up soon after doing the five-day commercials. You see, they were looking for a model with limpid eyes and a sultry mouth."

Yang the cat and Sasha the dog would soon become part of a split family. Barbara divorced husband Lucien to marry, just two years later, *Get Smart* production manager Burt Nodella. She remained Agent 86 for the duration, from 1965 to 1970, and in 1968 and 1969 was nominated for an Emmy as Outstanding Lead Actress in a Comedy Series. While her on-camera acting parts dwindled away, she began doing voice-over commercials on a vast scale, and she has continued to enjoy her lifestyle.

ED PLATT (*GET SMART*)
Pow-Wow Time With the Chief...
Can He Maintain Control Over 86?

Off camera, Ed Platt is feeling no pain. His role in *Get Smart* as The Chief (or Agent Q in a few episodes) of CONTROL, an organization of spies, has brought him more fame than all the character roles he has played over the years in Broadway productions and such major feature films as *Rebel Without a Cause* and *North By Northwest*.

Last season (1965-1966), *Get Smart* became a much-discussed spoof on the spy genre. Its comedy characteristics (as conceived by Buck Henry and Mel Brooks) inspired a book of *Would You Believe It?* gags, the name for a New York nitery, a seasonal card depicting Santa Claus speaking into his shoe telephone, and sundry items suitable for commercial exploitation. I believe it's called Merchandising, or Let's Make a Buck Off Whatever Is Popular!

Ed, accustomed to the anonymity of an actor who never fully attains stardom though his roles may number in the hundreds, suddenly found himself associated with all that popularity—despite his initial belief that his part as the stone-faced straight man who must bear the brunt of Smart's idiocy and tomfoolery was "just another part" to tide him over for a while.

Although the commercial aspects have by now run their course, *Get Smart* has not changed its satiric formula, and many critics have praised it for remaining consistently witty. Platt, however, has certain reservations. "I don't think we've been so sustaining," he insists. "It is terribly difficult to top 'Would you believe it!' and 'Sorry about that, Chief,' every week. I think we established too strong a precedent early on and have failed to surpass it, which is what we should do if we're all that good."

How does Platt see the character of Chief as he relates to Smart? "Certainly I'm a foil, a frustration symbol, a wall of stone off which Max can bounce his humor. And naturally I'm bordering on psychosis—I would have to be with a guy like Max hanging

Ed Platt aka The Chief on Get Smart.

around all the time. While Agent 99 [Barbara Feldon] serves as a Mother Image, I guess you could say I am the forgiving Father, always willing to turn the other cheek and give my 'son' just one more chance.

"As for Max, he represents the universal idiocy of Man. He says to the world, 'Look, I'm stupid' (which mankind is doing all the time whether it knows it or not), bumbles his way into a dangerous situation, adds 'But not that stupid,' or 'I asked you not to tell me that,' and emerges triumphant. The only difference in real life is—we don't always come out so clean."

While most Hollywood sound stages tend to be tedious places to visit, the *Get Smart* sets at a branch of the Paramount Studios offer a rare and welcome diversion, for Ed and Don Adams take great pleasure in ribbing each other during rehearsals, their non-scripted show often funnier than anything that might turn up on the home screen.

Dick Curd, NBC's Hollywood press agent for *Get Smart*, tells me, "Ed's deep voice has supplied him with authoritative roles over the years. He's been cast as district attorneys, sheriffs, lawyers, and similar types in more films than even he can remember. He has steadily gone up, up, up–but he is not star material and can only attain certain plateaus.

"With *Get Smart*, he has finally been elevated into a position his experience warrants. Unlike some people around here, Ed hasn't lost his perspective. He's a humble man, and he doesn't believe he is as important as the rest of the cast. The others are the real stars and he knows this. Still, he is the key straight man and as essential as anyone in contributing to the show's content."

Ed says, "I'm about a thousand miles short of being a genius in my profession. I always have been, always will be. I started out studying to be the world's great bass singer. Coaching, lessons—I went through the whole thing at the Juilliard School of Music and the Cincinnati Conservatory of Music.

"But all I had to show for it after a few years were (1) many holes in my shoes, (2) a sore throat, and (3) the belated knowledge that actors were making a helluva lot more money than I was. So I decided to make the change to stage and radio, and subsequently to films and TV."

Because of the popularity of the Chief, Platt has been prodded into accepting a number of nightclub and county fair bookings around the country during a break in filming. What kind of act does he have in mind?

"Actually," he tells me, "there's nothing in my mind at the moment. My agent called me just the other day, asked me if I wanted to do it, and I said, 'Sure. Why not?' I'm excited—no, I'm scared. I haven't done a solo act in years. I feel like a child who's just been discovered holding a stick of dynamite with a smoking fuse. I know what emotion I can evoke from an audience with my singing, and I'll throw in some humor (e.g. my shoe can suddenly ring like a telephone). Anyone who can't identify with the voice can identify with the series. But I keep worrying about my voice . . . it's been so long since I belted a song. As Max might say, 'You better find that voice, or you're gonna be in a lotta trouble, fella.'"

Platt completed 133 episodes of *Get Smart* before moving on in 1970 to play Orrin Hacker in the short-lived comedy series, *The Governor and J.J.* Platt raised the money for producer Deno Paoli to shoot the Glenn Ford film, *Santee*, completely on videotape in 1973, a move that might have led to financial problems and a state of depression. Some believe that Platt's death in 1974 at the age of fifty-eight was preceded by two failed suicide attempts, so the cause of death remains shrouded in uncertainty.

DON ADAMS (*GET SMART*)
More Dozy Than Nosy: The Day Agent 86 Arrived in San Francisco on a New Mission

Don Adams (with Barbara Feldon) holding his shoe-telephone that became an oft-repeated gag on Get Smart. Call it sole-searching.

8:30 in the morning at the Southern Pacific depot at Third and Townsend in San Francisco is a good place to bump into swarms of scurrying commuters, including Don Adams. He disembarks to be greeted by a cloudless sky. He stands alone for a moment on the platform, sucking in a mouthful of fresh air, his eyes concealed behind dark glasses. Is he perhaps spying on someone? Hmm . . . .

Although instantly recognizable as the actor who has made Maxwell Smart (maybe better known to some as Agent 86) into a new kind of absurd American hero through the *Get Smart* comedy series, Don is an unimposing figure, short in height, and clad in a glen plaid suit set off by a red dress shirt with matching vest and tie.

He looks tired, and this he immediately admits. "I didn't sleep much last night. I'd just doze off." A hand motion simulates a bouncing sleeper. "Then, I'd be shaken awake again." He begins the short walk to the street, a redcap following with his luggage. "I've got this hang-up about flying. Had four bad experiences a few years ago. On the fifth trip, I was flying from Mexico to New York, when all four engines conked out at once. As I was hurtled earthward, I swore I'd never fly again. I survived that one, but I'm beginning to think it's better to go down in flames than to be rattled to death."

Waiting for Don in front of the station is a personable publicity man, Dick Skuse, who handles personalities for Harrah's Club in Reno, which is Don's ultimate destination. The TV series has brought him so much notoriety that he is now a comedy star, appearing in showrooms around the country. Ironically, being a stand-up comedian is how he started out in show business, and hence you might say he's back where he started. Only now, one might add, there's a brighter glow around his body.

Skuse motions for us to jump into a waiting limousine. As we climb into the backseat, Don points to the book he has been carrying, *The Best of Jim Murray*. "One of the funniest sports writers I've ever read," he says, tapping the cover. "I class him with Red Smith and Jimmy Cannon. This guy, Murray, not only can write but he does it with a grand sense of humor. Listen." Don turns to a certain page and reads, "'The first time you look at [champion boxer] Sonny Liston, you only hope he doesn't bite.' See what I mean?"

Don becomes distracted as the limousine crosses Market Street and begins the ascent up Nob Hill. His gaze is concentrated on pedestrians and buildings, but his mind seems somewhere else. Or is he once again spying on the people of San Francisco in an effort to help CONTROL carry out some new citizen-protection program?

Why hasn't he brought his wife and child with him? "Oh, they prefer to fly. They'll meet me later in Reno, after I open in Harrah's Headliner Room."

Hasn't he even brought an agent with him from Los Angeles?

"Listen," he says, grimacing, "the trip on the train alone was bad enough. Don't suggest anything that would make it worse."

How has the weather been in Los Angeles?

"I wouldn't know. I've spent the last four weeks in Vegas playing the Sands Hotel. Didn't do badly in the Tony Lema Memorial Tournament. I'm a real golf fan." He again gazes pensively through the window.

Say, hadn't he served with the U.S. Marines in the Pacific?

"Yes, Guadalcanal. I got shot up. Came down with malaria. I spent a year in hospital. Once I was back on my feet, I was a drill instructor. You know, all that painful stuff seems so long ago. It's hard to realize it all happened in this lifetime. So long ago...."

The limousine pulls into the entrance to the Fairmont Hotel, and within two minutes, Don's luggage has been checked, along with the Murray book and his attaché case. The check-in clerk tells him that the suite reserved in his name is still being occupied by steel magnate Roger Blau. Would Mr. Adams mind terribly taking a smaller room until the matter can be cleaned up? A shrug indicates Adams couldn't care less. Perhaps some breakfast? "Yeah, coffee," he says, "black coffee." We head for the Camellia Room.

Once seated, and a filled coffee cup is before him, Don sips intently from the cup, and I decide it's time to learn all I can about *Get Smart*. That is, Don, if another interview about your show isn't too much of a drag.

He permits one of his few smiles. "Naw, I don't mind. It's like everything else. It depends on how you feel at the moment. Right now I'm sleepy, that's all. That train ride, all night long. A drag."

First off, what does he attribute to the series' success?

"I think it was the combined comedy genius of three guys: Leonard Stern, Buck Henry, and Mel Brooks, who all helped in creating *Get Smart*. Their timing was good for a spy spoof. So was my timing. I just happened to be around when they needed an actor whose style suited the character of Max.

"After all, Max is almost identical with the character of the house detective I did on *The Bill Dana Show* for three years. I played this stumbling, fumbling house detective named Byron Glick. Would you believe that bit was originally a take-off on William Powell's 'Thin Man'?

Across the table, Skuse, who has been unobtrusive as he flips through the pages of the morning *San Francisco Chronicle*, suddenly springs to life to tell us that *Get Smart* has been nominated for an Emmy Award. So has Don Adams in the Best Male Comedy Star category.

Don reacts with genuine surprise. "Hey, I didn't know that." He grabs the Entertainment section from Skuse's grasp and peruses the story quickly. "Hmmm . . . very nice. I'm really pleased." He puts the paper down and sips more coffee, the brightest smile on his face yet this morning.

"I've worked nightclubs most of my life," he contributes voluntarily. "For fourteen years, I played the strip clubs, the worst kind of joints imaginable, even if some of the joints they show are pleasing to the eye. It used to be I'd do my set bits, my routines. Detectives, district attorneys, umpires. But now, because of TV, people are more knowledgeable comedy-wise. You've got to relate more directly to them; they're no longer satisfied with what you might call 'canned' material. They want something fresh.

"That's why I've changed my nightclub style in just the last few years. Now everything is conversational, you talk to your audience. They become part of what's happening."

How would he classify himself among comedians in general?

"I'm too inhibited to be a great comedian. Steve Allen once said, 'You can only be as great as you dare to be.' I don't dare that much on the stage or nightclub floor. My biggest asset is my comedy timing. For me to extend beyond that, I would have to develop my understanding of the rhythm and flow of comedy material.

I would not get a signed photo from Don Adams until 1975 when I interviewed him for his new series, Don Adams' Screen Test, *in which contestants would re-enact famous scenes from memorable motion pictures.*

Don yawns anew. Skuse reads to him a list of upcoming interviews and appointments that will have him busy all day. "If you don't mind," says Adams, "I've got thirty minutes before the next interview. I think I'll duck upstairs and grab some sleep. That damn train ride . . . ."

Get Smart continued through 1970, totaling five seasons. In all, Don was nominated four times for an Emmy and won three. After that, he hosted a show he created himself, *Don Adams' Screen Test*, but it lasted only for one season in syndication. He went back to doing voice-overs for the *Inspector Gadget* animated series, and then in 1995 came back in a new twist on his old show, still called *Get Smart*, only then he portrayed the head of CONTROL and had to "control" the wild antics of his son Max Jr., portrayed by Andy Dick. It failed to connect and lasted for only seven episodes.

Don (birth name Donald James Yarmy) died in 2005 at the age of seventy-two of lung disease.

PAT PAULSEN
Alive and Levitating in Hollywood With Two Brothers He Smothers With Comedy

I was invited to attend a rehearsal of *The Smothers Brothers Comedy Hour*, with the intent not to interview the brothers but to meet Pat Paulsen, a comedian that had become a familiar face on the show.

The Smothers Brothers had first premiered their act at the Purple Onion in 1959, demonstrating a musical ability, as the elder brother, Tom (or "Tommy"), played the acoustic guitar and Dick (or "Dickie") played the string bass. They also had a comic patter, in which Tommy was the jokester and Dick was the straight man. Their first TV attempt in 1965-1966, *The Smothers Brothers Show*, a sitcom in which Tom played an angel down on planet Earth taking care of out-of-control but-still-alive brother Dick, was a ratings failure.

The Smothers Brothers Comedy Hour debuted in 1967 and soon after became one of the most controversial series in the history of television, up to that time. The boys' humor, and the comments made by some liberal-minded guests, began to touch sexual issues, anti-Vietnam War sentiments, religious beliefs, and, perhaps the most upsetting to the CBS network at the time, civil rights (or racial) issues. Include in all of that repeated jabs and right-crosses to the very jaw of the then-in-power Nixon Administration.

In early October 1967, I met Pat Paulson in the series' early months, before the controversy began. He and I came smashing together, and got a little smashed in the process. Here it is:

Pat says, "I've got this editorial," and he tries to beam with pride. Like most of his facial expressions, it goes **SPLAT!**

Seated in the rehearsal hall at CBS Television City, surrounded by a production team, leotard-clad dancers and Tommy and Dickie, Pat's voice becomes momentarily lost in the overwhelming volume of a rock 'n roll group, The Association, as it goes through its

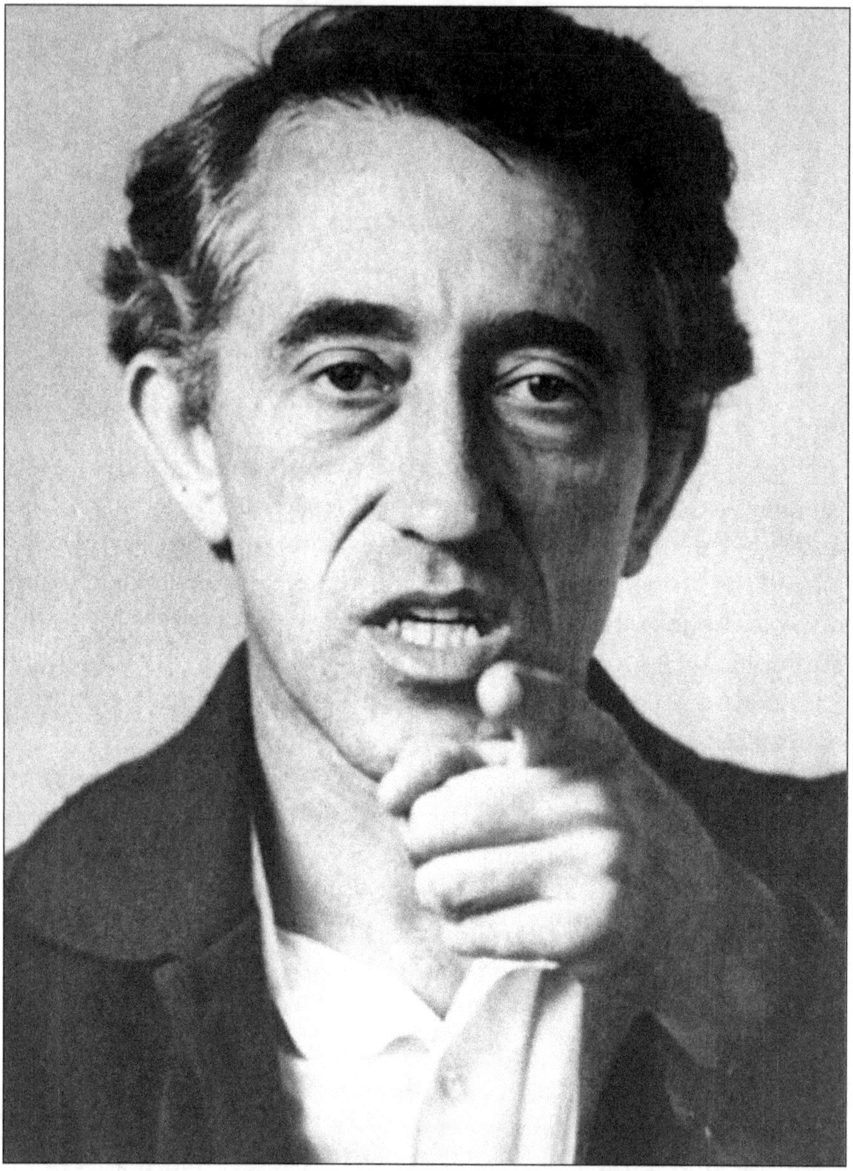

Pat Paulsen

paces two days before actual taping for the next episode. Finally, there is a decline in the din. Pat unfurls a sheet of paper and opens his mouth to explain the editorial's contents.

   The hand of famed British actress Greer Garson lies heavily on his shoulder. He stares up into her smile with the eyes of a basset hound contemplating the moon. An exchange of introductions, then Greer—guest star of the week—floats off through the rehearsal hall as if lost. "Now there's a Grand Old Actress," says Paulsen.

I agree with him, mentioning her great roles as Madame Curie and as Mrs. Miniver.

He snaps back to the subject. "Remember now, the story you're writing is about me. This week's editorial. It's about doctors." He gives me a private reading. It is typically Pat Paulsen material, delivered in a dry voice that makes a mockery of dramatic impact.

At the age of forty, his elongated face is lifeless; the bags under his eyes droop double-fold; his lips, already thin and pushed in, seem to grow even thinner, more pushed in; his eyelids sag a lot.

Does he need a nudge to keep from falling asleep?

No. There is that nervous little chuckle. Pat, you see, is awake, alive, and living in Hollywood, "smother-ing all" with his unusual comedy!

Finished with the satirical editorial, Pat assumes full attentiveness (equivalent to a brown bear rolling over in December). For some inexplicable reason, he suddenly becomes self-conscious about his dress: gold-colored pants, an amber shirt, and loafers. "This," he apologizes, "is not a dress rehearsal." He wiggles uncomfortably. "Underneath, I'm covered with hickies." At the end of the table, a dancer in leotards lets out a gasp and drops her soft drink bottle.

Charming Greer Garson whirls delightfully through a wildly insane Scottish skit with the Smothers Brothers, then it is Pat's turn. He unfurls his piece of paper, sits down, clears his throat with an authoritative "Hmmmmmmmm-Hrrmmmmm," and delivers the editorial, his weekly shtick, in his usual deadpan manner. About doctors.

Afterwards, he confers with an Official-Looking Type. Gloom scuds over his face as he shambles back to the rehearsal table. He shrugs. "The editorial is gonna be cut. To ribbons. They say the show is running too long. I think it's the dancers that are too long—legged, I mean. Who around here wants to start a running battle with management? I don't wanna go back to selling door-to-door like I used to."

But hey, I tell him, isn't that where you got the deadpan?

He nods, "Yeah, of course."

(This whittling away is nothing new to him. His editorials have often been censored by CBS, just as much as the Smothers Brothers' material has been axed at the last minute. CBS should hold its breath—those execs ain't seen nothin' yet.)

He tells me he has a strong walk-on bit in a barber shop comedy routine, so all is not lost. His "millions of fans will still yock it up." He now adds, "Let's get out of here before they cut me out of the barber shop gang. It's called clipping."

Across the street from CBS Television City, Pat takes his ease over a drink in an air-conditioned bar-restaurant thriving on early evening action. The atmosphere is pleasant and it seems to remove some of the tension from his demeanor, apparent since his negative conference with the Official-Looking Type. Pat even makes a derogative crack at a CBS censor who is sitting at the bar counter. The censor laughs back whole-heartedly. In his eyes: Try that on the air, buddy.

Pat perks up and orders a lobster-oriented dinner. He gives off a mild "Burp!" as the waiter scurries away. Pat wanders, "They say I got talent but they never say anything about my body. Charlie Chaplin is a genius. I've seen *City Lights* ten times. Pantomime king." To prove it, Pat doesn't move a muscle in his body, but does roll his eyeballs slightly, keeping his face the usual deadpan.

I ask him how he first conceived the editorial concept.

A knowing smile, an intimate clutching of my arm. "You're from San Francisco, my home stomping grounds." From beneath the table comes the sound of stomping feet. "So you're going to know what I'm talking about. So will your readers. There's one Bay Area TV station that is always running serious-minded editorials delivered by one of its executives. I think he's still doing them today. In fact, I always got a kick out of his 'style' and decided to adopt it, focusing in on some of his more fallible areas."

He suddenly changes the subject. "I levitate," he says in total seriousness. "Have ever since I served with the Marines during World War II."

During?

"Well, shortly thereafter."

I learn that he did, after the war, spend time guarding Japanese prisoners of war. He spreads a few grains of salt on the tail of his lobster. "Besides levitation, I do yogi."

You mean yoga?

"Oh no, I've never done that in my life. Strictly yogi. Bear with me!" He bursts out laughing. He just cannot, he explains, restrain himself, and he gets back to his "love of levitation."

I make a joke. Would he care to drift over to the bar to demonstrate his uplifting abilities?

A dissenting movement of his head. "I can levitate only in private. Funny thing, but can't do it when others are around. Especially newspaper guys from San Francisco."

That seems very funny. A pleasant put-on that's urbane, witty, controversial.

"It's no put-on," he reprimands. "I levitate. Period."

Pat begins to look with distrust over his half-eaten lobster tail.

Is something wrong?

"I don't trust you fellas. Newspapermen, I mean. You guys write things I don't especially like. What are *you* going to write?"

I tell him, "The very things you've been saying. What I see, what I hear."

"Oh, that's good," he says. "I respect honesty. Oh, be sure to tell your readers I'm the World's Greatest Comedian—with all the capital letters."

Pat takes an extra-heavy bite of lobster to emphasize his next point. "I'm also a painter. I tie myself onto the ceiling and drop face-down onto the canvas. I paint with my face: The Nose Dab, the Jaw Swirl, the Ear Flick. I call it the Swing Thrust, or the Free Face Style. I've created myriad forms of abstract art. I sell them to kids at auctions."

Another put-on? I hesitate in my judgment. It is a recorded fact that he first face-painted what is called *The Last Days of Mussolini* on a sidewalk in Vancouver, British Columbia.)

Supper over, Pat suggests we adjourn to the Ice House, a popular nightclub in Pasadena. He played there often before the Smothers Brothers gave him his big break in TV, and now that he's in the Big Time, he " . . . hasn't forgotten who his friends are."

Often, without warning anybody, he returns to the Ice House to "... try out my editorials." Tonight, he is in the mood for just that.

The Ice House, thirty minutes of freeway traffic later, turns out to be similar to San Francisco's Purple Onion in atmosphere and decor, but the audience appears to be a different age bracket. Most of the crowd is composed of aging teenie-boppers drinking pink lemonade and apple cider. Ties and high heels are definitely not part of this scene.

As we drink at least two beers, the acts we see are improvised, casual, a soothing relief after the freeway and dense night fog. Pat talks up each act in advance. He knows these cats, having worked with them back in the " . . . hard times," when he was "struggling for fame and fortune."

Obviously, he is nervous.

Could it be stage fright despite the fact he is viewed by millions each Sunday night?

He shrugs, then jumps up and hurries out into the lobby for another beer, another chat with a patron. Good for the image, mingling.

Finally, Pat returns, a copy of the editorial that was recently cancelled from the show once again rolled up in his hand. Now it is his turn to perform. A sound effects comedian introduces Pat and shyly he makes his way to the stage. Under the subdued stage lighting, it is difficult to tell whether he is blushing or not. He unfurls the familiar piece of paper and faces the expectant audience.

"I've got this editorial . . . ."

Pat Paulsen found greater fame as a deadpan comic when, just a few weeks after we met, the Smothers Brothers allowed him to take on the role of a presidential candidate running for the STAG Party (Straight Talking American Government). It will be his most memorable moment, and it is reminiscent of Gracie Allen's 1940 run for presidency as a rep of the Surprise Party. Pat had his own series in 1969, *Pat Paulsen's Half-an-Hour Comedy Hour*, but it lasted only thirteen weeks. He continued doing the presidential/political satire for many years, and died of colon cancer in 1997 at the age of sixty-nine. I will always remember him for his ability to make fun of himself in an ad libbed manner.

Pat Paulsen during the period when he "ran" for the presidential office on The Smothers Brothers Comedy Hour. *Paulsen was representing the Stag Party.*

THE SMOTHERS BROTHERS
Lower Billings for the Smothers, Maybe, But the Boys Are Glad To Be Active Akin Again

Meanwhile, back at CBS Television City, *The Smothers Brothers Comedy Hour* becomes one of the hottest shows in the public media. As far as CBS is concerned, it is heat it doesn't like, and it works on the Smothers Brothers to cool it. They ignore their request, and the series keeps getting more attention, but the wrong kind as far as CBS is concerned. Finally, at the end of the fourth season, the Smothers Brothers are literally fired and their series is cancelled. Even if they will never hit a height of popularity like that again, they have implanted themselves upon the American culture, and have helped to change the morality code that dominates movies and TV.

They continue performing together and as solo acts. That's when I finally come along to interview them in November 1981. The team is scheduled to perform at the San Jose Center for the Performing Arts, so the *San Francisco Chronicle* wants an update.

Tommy, who lives in what he calls "a modest home" in Sonoma County's Kenwood, is away in Hollywood guest starring in an episode of *The Love Boat*, so I speak with him by phone. ("*Love Boat*, he tells me, "isn't important, but developing one's acting skills is!")

Dick, who lives in the Santa Cruz mountains and is hoping to establish a new winery business, is available. We meet at Bardelli's Restaurant in the city. Beside me are Tommy's quotes that I took over the phone, because I want to see if Dick agrees or disagrees with his brother's philosophies.

The Smothers Brothers never broke up the duo back in 1976; they simply told their agent they wanted to stop the nightclub, concert, and Tahoe-Vegas circuits so they could test their skills individually in other venues. Their farewell show as a standup team was at Harrah's Tahoe in October 1976.

Tom and Dick Smothers

Producers, however, didn't congregate backstage to sign up either of the boys as they finished that final performance. As Dick Smothers recalls, "At that time, there was no demand for stand-up musician-comedians outside the circuits we'd been working in. No need for two funny guys."

Tom recollects, "We wanted to go out as individuals and see what we had . . . but opportunities were just as limited."

For a while, Tom was appearing in movies, such as *The Silver Bears* with Louis Jourdan, *The Serial* with Martin Mull, and *There Goes the Bride* with Twiggy. Dick was doing dinner theater and establishing that winery, a life-long dream. Tom remembers those days well because "people could never make the separation in their minds. They'd see me and ask, 'Where the hell is your brother?' It made me realize in retrospect that all the things we'd done that we liked, we'd done together. And we gravitated back toward each other."

It still wasn't the old nightclub act, though. They appeared on Broadway in 1979 in the musical bedroom farce, *I Love My Wife*, which toured five months before closing in San Francisco in 1980. They also teamed to star in a six-part TV miniseries, *Fitz and Bones*, about a reporter-and-cameraman team working for a San Francisco TV station. Tom recalls, "It didn't fare very well. It had a couple of good episodes and a couple of poorly-written episodes. Of course, our acting was great!" Cancellation resulted.

Last year, the boys re-teamed as a musical-comedy duo for two NBC specials and told their agent they wanted to get back into the nightclub world. Since then, they've been the opening act for headliners, but they're switching the tables now to appear as headliners in San Jose in a few days with Shields & Yarnell as their warm-up act.

Now it is lunchtime at Bardelli's, and Dick is eagerly putting away plenty of food.

"Dick, I spoke with your brother just a few hours ago about your original act, and he's excited as hell about doing it again. He told me how you first presented it as the Purple Onion in '59. That's my favorite nightclub—small, intimate, where I was the first to interview Jim Nabors."

"I love that place, too," says Dick, still eating eagerly. "You go down the stairs into that compact place. Who would have thought you could start a career down in that darkness?"

I continue, "Tommy, he was hoping you weren't dinosaurs with the old act, but then he said that your experience in theater and TV had taught you improved timing, and that the old act should seem fresh and alive, different because nobody else does comedy quite like you guys. Agree?"

"Yeah, yeah," says Dick, putting down his fork and knife. "For a while, we did warm-up acts for Lola Falana, John Davidson, Shecky Greene, Glen Campbell, and Tony Orlando, adding new routines as we went. Not a comedown, playing second bananas to a star. We'd do about forty minutes and get the crowd really revved up. And that's great for the headliner, because it's better to come out to a hot audience than a cold one."

I tell Dick, "Here's something else Tommy told me: 'It feels real good to go out and perform. We finish and we don't have that responsibility of being the headliners. We can watch the rest of the show, go have dinner or go see another show if we're in Vegas. There's not all that pressure on us like we used to feel.'"

Dick nods. "It's like starting all over again. A second chance."

"Something else Tommy told me, Dick. He said, 'I always think I'm losing it. I wake up some mornings and feel basically insecure. I'm only happy when I'm working. All careers are based on ebb and flow, and right now we're flowing.' Do you feel like you're flowing?"

Dick sips half a glass of water. "Upriver sometimes, but always flowing. Whatever our indulgences over the years, we try to look youthful and healthy, not like two middle-aged guys. We've been accused of being predictable, but so is Bob Hope. When you change your style, that's when you lose your identity and go downhill."

I say, "Tom told me that audiences relate to family. They can sense a more personal intimacy between relations. Your spontaneous thought process is that you're brothers; you couldn't possibly have rehearsed the kind of put-down jokes you exchange. And that when you started at the Onion, you didn't follow any current trend. Nobody had influenced you. You learned to be funny together through your music. You found rhythm."

Dick almost jumps out of his chair. "What a brother! I've always felt we were a success, not because of our talent, for we're marginally talented, but because of the combination of our personalities and the way we worked together. Plus universal subject matter with real longevity.

"Take my brother, for example. He remains the world's worst bass player after twenty-three years. He has the native ability to say something wrong correctly and make it funny. You need that native ability to last. You can refine your craft, but you can never be taught to be funny, say the way that Robin Williams is funny.

"Tommy," continues Dick, "has body language and he's more important to the act. I'm an ideal complement to him. I'm not so good without him. I'm the straight man and can't get his laughs. I give Tommy input and he spins off from that. Tommy's always been the mothered kind. Grandmothers, mothers, little girls. To them he's a loveable little creature who's the underdog. He's not a wimp; he's sympathetic."

"Hey, here's something Tommy told me. His advice to would-be comedians, a question I often ask. He said, 'Don't get too prepared and don't let your material show. Make it seem personal, natural.'"

"Good advice. Naturalness is the key."

"I asked Tommy about his future plans, his hope for tomorrow."

"What'd that guy tell you?"

"Let's see . . . yeah, he said, 'I just want to work on the act. Records aren't important. Film and TV are secondary. We're not pressing it. We're not trying to prove a point. We're not heating up an old career; we're starting a whole new one. It feels good, it feels real good.'"

"That's Tommy. My future? I re-evaluated my goals recently and realized I don't have any goals. But, will I now attain the goals I don't want and will I be happy with them? Goals restrict you. One shouldn't use goals because then when you reach them, you have to set another goal. In this business, you can't plan or choreograph events to come. You'll only frustrate yourself. You have to be ready for anything that comes along."

After 1981, the Smothers Brothers gave non-stop performances in a variety of media through 2010, when they officially retired with a final show in Las Vegas. They ran the Remick Ridge Vineyards, a winery in Sonoma County, California. In 2003, the brothers were given the George Carlin Freedom of Expression Award, in "support of the First Amendment." No doubt this was in memory of their 1967-1969 TV series and its ahead-of-its-time attempt to break down the barriers of taboo that existed during that era. It is for this show, no matter how controversially it touched the

American viewing audience, that the Smothers Brothers will always be most remembered. Me, I'll always think of them as two young guys who walk down the steps of the Purple Onion, look around and one says, "So this is where show business begins for us...."

MARY TYLER MOORE
CBS Names New Show After Wife of TV Comedy Writer

In the beginning, there is *The Dick Van Dyke Show* (1961-1966), with Mary Tyler Moore portraying Laura, the wife of a TV comedy writer (Dick Van Dyke). In 1965, she is awarded a Golden Globe for her role. Beginning in 1970, she has a show of her own. Ever convinced of her fame, CBS names it after her, just as they did for Dick Van Dyke.

Movie cameras swoosh across the sound stage, narrowly avoiding any number of collisions. It seems like some kind of magical co-ordination that doesn't seem possible given the burly men that muscle the dollies to and fro. Cameramen press their eyeball sockets faithfully against their viewfinders, following the action of the performers. Above them, men on catwalks dip and swing their microphones, always stopping short of disastrous crashes against male and female hairdos.

To the casual observer, it looks like routine, run-of-the-mill, everyday Hollywood film production work. Actually, the cameras don't have any film in their magazines, the soundman is reading the latest *Playboy* instead of working his controls, and the gum that Mary is chewing with the jaw action of Bugs Bunny loose in a carrot patch is definitely not in the script.

All this is really a rehearsal for one of the installments to be filmed for *The Mary Tyler Moore Show*, which is now in its third season on CBS. It is December 1972, and we are at CBS Studio Center in North Hollywood, where Gene Autry and Roy Rogers once rode against the forces of evil in the American West when it was Republic Studios. Mary, her co-stars, and that well coordinated crew will go through five hectic days to get a single half-hour of entertainment on celluloid.

Work on the show begins on Monday with a plain rehearsal, during which the performers have the opportunity to try out various nuances and the writers can rewrite if things don't go

Mary Tyler Moore at the height of her TV career.

smoothly. Tuesday and Wednesday will be spent blocking out the action, set by set. Thursday will be devoted to blocking out camera movements, microphone placements, final set dressings, etc.

On Friday evening, an audience will be ushered in (bleachers are being conveniently provided) and the cast and crew will do their thing as one continuous stage play with the added spontaneity of warm bodies and uncanned applause.

Mary, a beanpole of a woman, is dressed this particular Thursday in pants, print blouse and sneakers—things she might wear in the garden to weed the begonias or trim the shrubs.

In addition to being an eager gum chewer, she is an active seat popper, being up and down like a jack-in-the-box with Mexican jumping beans lodged in its system. Her enthusiasm, a kind of bubbling, youthful effervescence, is in full evidence. The $25,500 Rolls Royce parked outside the sound stage may be hers, but she has yet to turn jaded; she has yet to lose that naive quality that made her so great as Dick Van Dyke's TV wife, Laura Petrie, and which now ranks her among the winners in the ratings game. (She has already won two Golden Globe Awards.)

As Mary plops down for the interview, plastic coffee cup in hand, there is no mistaking her preoccupation with the job at hand. Although she is eager to return to the rehearsal, she somehow erases it all from her mind for this moment of one-on-one and begins radiating her charms.

"More and more people are beginning to agree with me that this is the way to film a TV series. Oh, obviously I don't mean the private eye shows; I mean for the indoor situation comedy, this is really preferable. It's a healthier, happier way of working because it gives us all extra time for each of us to exploit our talents."

Mary acknowledges that her series, which debuted in 1970, has been successful, and has a little more to offer than *The Brady Bunch,* if you don't mind the comparison. She accredits James Brooks and Allan Burns with the concept (wide-eyed girl comes to Minneapolis-St. Paul to work in the news department of a TV station and is hired as an associate producer for *The Six O'clock News*) but more with its characters, such as the slave-driving news editor, the prissy newscaster, and Mary's man-starved roommate.

From this format, and from *The Dick Van Dyke Show,* Mary has assumed, in the public's eye, a certain wholesome image. "I don't think people really think of me in those terms. I think they realize I lead a totally different life away from TV. People are far more sophisticated today than we sometimes give them credit for being. I think they've come to respect and appreciate some of the things they're getting on the tube."

Mary lives with her husband, TV producer Grant Tinker, in a beach house in Malibu. She calls it a "giant sandbox" where she unwinds and gets away from the grind. "Friday night, after we complete a filming here, we go to a nearby saloon and talk about the show and then we start to climb down off our acting boxes. That's the one reward I look forward to each week. That and Malibu, and Tinker, of course."

Between the time of the cancellation of the Dick Van Dyke series and the beginning of her own show, things did not go swimmingly for Mary. Her films at Universal (*Run a Crooked Mile, Thoroughly Modern Millie*, among others) left her very unsatisfied, and her experience of doing the play, *Holly Golightly*, which ran into production problems and closed before it opened, still causes her to shudder.

"However," she admits, "I think it was beneficial to go through that period. Sometimes things can go so well you lose all perspective of yourself, and you become something you really aren't. I think we need adversity to grow. And I do want to grow. I never want to stop learning about this business."

Someone signals Mary to return to the stage. "You know," she says apologetically, "this is one of those days when we're still hashing out several problems. I pray for only one thing on a day like this: 'Please God, don't let me forget my lines.'"

After she has crumbled up her coffee cup and returned to her place, the cameras begin swooshing back and forth, and up in the catwalks, men are dipping and swinging their microphones... and life goes on for Mary Tyler Moore.

Mary's sitcom continued through 1977 and became a highly acclaimed program, topping the list of best-watched shows. It received Emmy Awards three years in a row (1975-1955), and Mary was nominated for six more Golden Globe Awards, and won a Golden Globe for her role in the film, *Ordinary People* (1980). As for Emmy Awards, she was nominated eleven times and won five. Two years ago, *The Mary Tyler Moore Show* was ranked #6 out of 101 Best Written Series of All Time.

VICKI LAWRENCE
Do You Remember Vicki, Who Transformed Into a Matriarch While Still in Her Thirties?

Vicki Lawrence's transformation is amazing because she uses so few accoutrements (and no makeup, no aging tricks at all) to affect the illusion. By simply donning a curly gray wig, a pair of wire-rimmed glasses, and a frumpy dress, she adds about forty years to her appearance. She instantly stops being a young Hollywood actress (at this very moment, age thirty-four) and is transfigured into Mama.

You remember Mama. Her prototype first appeared on *The Carol Burnett Show* in comedy sketches. Young, fresh-out-of-high-school Vicki, discovered in 1967 because she looked and sounded so much like Carol, had begun by playing her sister in some comedy sketches.

Beverly Archer as Iola Boylan and Vicki Lawrence as matriarch Thelma Harper on Mama's Family.

She quickly graduated to other comedy characters and finally to Eunice's mother, a fidgety old codger that fussed and stewed while the younger generation underwent its troubles and traumas.

Her Mama characterization shouldn't have worked more than once, yet it did. Audiences were willing to suspend disbelief, possibly because Vicki's satire of an oldster (complete with quavering voice) was something everyone could relate to. Who hasn't had a simpering mother-in-law, over-caring mother, or some variation on the meddling, aggressive little old lady in tennis shoes at some time in life? Such a target becomes an easy victim of our slings and arrows. There's also an aspect of love here, for we all tend to adore the grandmotherly image. Thus, Vicki's Mama gives us reminders of these conflicting stereotypes.

Only a month before February 1983, *Mama's Family* marked the return of the septuagenarian in a comedy series that portrays her with a whole new fictional family. Vicki has fine-honed the character after working several years with Harvey Korman on timing, dialects, and accents. "Harv taught me shtick, but above all else he taught me my craft," Vicki tells me, ensconced in a booth at Hamburger Hamlet in Beverly Hills, just days after her new comedy series has debuted on NBC.

"And now Mama is somebody greater than life, a character who can do all the things I can't do. She can cuss with a sailor from San Pedro and get away with it. She can storm around and make things unpleasant for everyone concerned. It's me and yet it's not me. My husband Al [Al Schultz], who used to work makeup on Carol's show, asks 'Who is that lady?' every time I scrub off my lipstick and rouge, remove my long eyelashes, and slip into that old dress.

"I look in the mirror and I wonder myself. Mama's fascinating to me. She's the only character I've ever played that doesn't make me nervous when I watch myself. I've always been critical of my every move, and yet I feel detached from Mama. Like she's someone else and I've never met her."

What, exactly, does make Mama tick?

"She's a strong, feisty matriarch, who loves her children too much and is always trying to save them from making fools of themselves. I see her as loving, tender, vulnerable, outspoken.

Cranky at times. Cantankerous at others. She's more colorful and multi-faceted; she isn't so headstrong or one-sided as she was on Carol's show. She isn't bickering all the time."

Mama had been such a strong character on the Burnett show that producer Joe Hamilton (who just happens to be Carol's husband) had wanted Vicki to do a series six years ago. "CBS had wanted the show and two writers were assigned to prepare a pilot. It was handed to me like a gift, but I had just had my first baby and I didn't feel like being an old lady every week. And I was very insecure, and kept asking myself: What if the show fails? I wanted to fly, not come home with my tail between my legs. It didn't feel right, so . . . I turned it down.

"You know, it's been said that all actors are children, and in a sense we are. Maybe some of us can't dress ourselves in the morning, yet to be professionals we must have an inbred instinct about what's right or wrong for us. We must trust our own judgments. And I trusted mine."

There were other factors. Vicki, who was born and raised in Inglewood, had grown up on Burnett's show, had met her husband-to-be there, and had her two children during that period. One day, she suddenly realized that her whole professional life had evolved around that one TV program, and those eleven years had been full ones: five Emmy nominations, and one Emmy for her work during the ninth season.

"Look," she says in her nervous, enthusiastic way, her voice still sounding like an intended parody of Carol Burnett, "the cast on that show was the last great ensemble in TV variety. Like graduating from Yale or Harvard with honors. Our peers respected us. I couldn't afford to go out and do junk. Carol had nurtured me and made me what I was. I owed it to her to make good. I just felt too uneasy to say yes to Joe."

Also, "I was twenty-eight when I realized I had never had time to spend with myself, to figure out who I was." Before her lay a personal odyssey that would lead her through four long, complicated years of restlessness.

The first step came when Vicki and husband, Al Schultz, sold their home and moved to the Hawaiian island of Maui with their two children, Courtney and Garrett. Gone was the freeway system, which Al hated, and everything Hollywood. Some people can live without its ambience, but Vicki began to grow uneasy out of sight and out of mind, as far as producers were concerned. Paradise turned sour within one year, and Vicki, feeling she had been forgotten, knew she had to return to Los Angeles, to be close to the work that was now in her blood.

Garry Marshall, one of the most successful producers in TV, offered her a specialty part in a one-hour *Laverne and Shirley*, which got the juices flowing again and led to a working friendship with Marshall. He wanted desperately to create a series for Vicki, but perhaps he was too desperate, for *Katmandu* still makes Vicki wrinkle her nose when she recalls it. "It had something to do with a bodyguard and a terrorist in a palace, where Vicki and her mother lived, but don't ask for details. And be thankful the networks passed on it."

More moving back and forth between L.A. and Maui led to anxiety attacks which clobbered Vicki. Her skin broke out in rashes. It was, according to her doctor, "midlife acne" caused by stress. Stress caused by indecision, by the fact that Marshall had come up with a second pilot that Vicki didn't like, in which she played three sisters: herself, a dumb blonde nightclub singer, and a nun. Marshall loved it and tried extra hard to make it work while Vicki felt a returning sense of uneasiness. In her eyes, there was no way the premise would ever work. Marshall refused to give it up and hired new writers to revise the concept. The rashes kept flaring up. Finally, even Marshall had to acquiesce, much to his regret, but not Vicki's.

The real luck came when *Eunice* was aired last year, a one-hour Carol Burnett special in which Vicki enacted Mama's death scene. Since we live in an age when the sequel to the first-time success is the rule rather than the exception, NBC decided to resurrect the old gal through *Mama's Family* in a format that now includes costars Betty White, Ken Berry, and Rue McClanahan.

"It's a big responsibility," says Vicki, who is now caught up in many phases of the show's production. "I had just come through that difficult period and I had to go from being a child dependent on others to being a father figure on whom others now rely. Harvey Korman is back with me to direct, and I think we're finally starting to settle down."

Vicki Lawrence signed this photo to "John and Erica, Much Love."

That doesn't mean that Vicki is now completely relaxed. "I didn't say I had settled down. I still have that stress problem. Maybe it'll go away next summer if the show is a hit and we get renewed. But I think I'm going to be living with it until then."

Mama's Family would prove to be a hit, remaining on the NBC network through 1985. Then it went into first-run syndication and that lasted until 1990, so Vicki Lawrence had quite a run.

HARVEY KORMAN
Lunch With Laughter Galore?
Not When the Main Dish Is Harvey Korman

Take a comedian to lunch and you might be in for some first-class entertainment. A jolly good time can be had with Dom De Luise, who simply refuses to put his mouth into the "off" position and subjects everybody in sight, including the guy who fills the water glasses, to his one-liners and frenzied, erratic sense of humor.

Rich Little will wile you with an hour filled with character impersonations, capturing such details as the way George Burns holds a cigar, the saddle weariness of John Wayne after a ten-hour ride on the trail, and how he might address a cactus plant, or the rugged independence of Humphrey Bogart, complete with voice impression. One's steak tends to grow cold–constant laughter tends to keep one from eating.

Take Harvey Korman to the King's Four-in-Hand Restaurant in Hollywood and you might think you're about to be regaled with wit and comedy, the ultimate in uproarious comedy. After all, Harvey has the reputation for being one of the funniest performers on TV, serving as second banana to Carol Burnett on her popular one-hour CBS series.

Harvey takes about thirty seconds to shatter any anticipation of non-stop laughter and merry mayhem. He arrives dressed as casually as you can get without going outside to work in the garden. He doesn't smile a heck of a lot, and he answers questions in a routine fashion, never trying to be cute or clever, just trying to give a decent, direct answer. You might say Harvey is Mr. Average Typical Ordinary. He's even balding a little, and he's pleasant to the waiter and the guy who fills the water glasses.

Sipping a Bloody Mary, he assumes an unassuming attitude. "I really look upon myself as an actor rather than a comedian. The writers give us a situation and the characters, and we then are required to bring them to life. Everybody talks about how Carol and I work together. I think you can call it chemistry. We have a

Harvey Korman, who signed this publicity photo to Erica.

cohesiveness, a common language, and goal. And we work fast, never getting in each other's way. That's what gives each *Carol Burnett Show* a special look, at least as I see it."

Many fans enjoy *The Carol Burnett Show* for its spontaneity, or seeming spontaneity. Harvey smiles one of his rare smiles and nods his head. "It's an indulgence to ad lib unless you've worked with somebody so long and have a rapport going. That's why we can break up, or deviate from the script, and still make it work to our advantage. The audience has come to expect a certain amount of that from us by now. We don't always go out of our way to offer it, but when it happens we let it happen, and it adds to the enjoyment of the show, for us and the audience."

It's hard to know what will work, continues Harvey. "The sketch may read good on paper, but getting it to breathe, that's the hard part. Our writers are organic writers. They don't write gags. They must have an honest premise to start with. If the framework is phony, the material quickly starts to fall flat."

Harvey, who has just turned forty-six this very month, first worked in TV with Danny Kaye in the early 1960s, and then shifted to Steve Allen in the summer of 1967 to do variety sketches. That same year he became Burnett's "leading man" when her series debuted.

While he was appearing in motion pictures on the side (*The Last of the Secret Agents*, *Lord Love a Duck*, and a few others he would rather forget), he was winning Emmy Awards for Outstanding Individual Achievement three years running.

Harvey is just as unassuming about awards, and immediately switches the subject. "Danny Kaye taught me that it's easy to do the predictable. And he was right. You have to take a chance to do the big things. That's how you develop your individuality as a performer."

Should *The Carol Burnett Show* be cancelled (and in the back of Harvey's mind there is always that fear) he has two "aces in the hole." One is TV directing, which he branched out into last year by directing two episodes of *The Dick Van Dyke Show*. The other is a standing deal with CBS for his own series. What would it be?

Harvey shrugs and refuses to let any cats out of his bag.

So, that's about it. Lunch with Harvey Korman. Unpretentious, relaxed, almost mundane, but it's nice to know that some comedians do occasionally unwind and forget about trying to be the

Funniest Man Alive. It's not the same as having a bit of food with De Luise or Little, nor not nearly as much fun, but it does seem a bit closer to reality.

Harvey Korman won another Emmy that very year we met. In 1975, he also won a Golden Globe for his comedy work with Carol Burnett. He was eventually joined in the popular series by Tim Conway, but no jealousy ever surfaced. In fact, the two appeared together on Conway's own TV series, and later they toured the country together to promote their film *The Longshot* (1986). They also made several straight-to-video films, and they toured in the play *The Odd Couple*. Harvey Korman died in 2008 at the age of eighty-one.

TIM CONWAY
Bumbling Tim Conway–Will He Stumble Playing an Oddball Private Eye?

In September 1982, Tim Conway is trying to portray a comedy version of Sam Spade or Richard Diamond, and maybe this isn't such a good time to be watching him on Stage 11 of Laird Studios, once the home base for producer David O. Selznick and the historic site where Atlanta burned in *Gone With the Wind*.

Conway, disguised as an old man with heavy makeup and a grayish wig, is standing in a workout treadmill and he's hanging onto a little old lady for dear life. The quaking machine is wildly out of control. The little old lady is a white-haired sweet thing in a pink robe (possibly from Pasadena), jiggling up and down with Conway as he tries to stop the contraption before it vibrates a few pounds off both of them. Conway's gray eyes are wild with fear, his face is contorted. He's fumbling clumsily for the control and behaving in a fashion that, for anyone who knows him, is not unbecoming to comedian Tim Conway.

That is to say, he is brightly alive as the wonderful bumbler we have come to recognize and love and laugh at through years of working in slapstick TV comedies and making such zany parodies as *The Shaggy D.A.* (1973). What's wrong with seeing him at his slaphappy klutz bug-eyed best?

Nothing, except that's exactly the image he doesn't want you to carry away if you're going to write about *Ace Crawford, Private Eye*. That's the moniker of the licensed shamus he plays and the title of his half-hour CBS sitcom that will debut in March 1983.

When Conway comes off the set, dripping with perspiration and wearing a khaki-colored bath robe, he seems more than slightly embarrassed.

"See," he starts to explain, almost fumbling his words as he fumbled with the little old lady, "this is going to be a change of pace for me. Ace Crawford is like nobody I've played before. This is not going to be the kind of broad humor I'm noted for. It's taken me twenty years to move to this character, and you came in on a scene that is not representative of the show. Someone is killing old folks in a retirement home and I've disguised myself to find the killer and almost just got killed myself."

Excuses, excuses! I think to myself. Talk about poor timing on the part of a journalist! Conway puts aside his mild embarrassment and makes himself readily available for an interview in a nearby dressing room. He thuds on a couch, crosses his legs and is all animation, as if brought to life by Walt Disney himself.

"This private eye, Crawford," he begins, his arms waving through the air like a signalman's, "is a guy who doesn't realize the dangers around him. He walks through them, not always comprehending the clues. Ace isn't the sharpest guy around, and always takes the wrong route. Still, he solves the mysteries in spite of himself.

"Now normally, a comedian is part of the physical action, but this calls for the opposite touch, a kind of restraint I'm not used to yet. I guess you'd call it no-reaction comedy. Deadpan stuff. Instinctively, I want to go wide-eyed and gape-mouthed, and maybe a little busy-talkative, but the director has to yell and remind me."

Crawford, trench-coated in the Raymond Chandler-style of the 1940s, with a bullet-riddled fedora slung low over his brow, "is a man of mystery," continues Conway, re-crossing his legs into a new direction, his body sagging slightly, as if he's trying to create a new character all his way just for my sake. "See, he comes out of a fogbank on a pier in some setting that has a Casbah feeling to it, the sardonic gleam of Humphrey Bogart in his eye. He never seems worried; I guess it's this quality of invulnerability that carries him through.

"Ace has no family, no office," Conway continues, dramatizing the imagery as if he is Dashiell Hammett incarnate. "A waterfront dive is his hangout. Women fall for him, but he's oblivious to their charms. Inch is the name of the bartender, a little guy played by Billy Barty, who's three feet, nine inches tall. Then, there's a blind piano player, that's Bill Henderson. And a sexy jazz singer, that's Shera Danese, and boy is she a knockout."

As Conway carries on, I cannot help but recall the Blake Edwards' series *Peter Gunn*, in which the private eye Gunn (Craig

Tim Conway in his guise as Ace Crawford, a TV private detective who lasted for all of five tough-man comedy adventures.

Stevens) visits a jazz club called Mother's, mainly to see the newest performance of "sexy jazz singer" Edie Hart, played by Lola Albright.

Conway again. "Dick Christie, he plays a flatfoot inspector, Lieutenant Fanning. Supposed to be a plainclothes cop, but he wears his badge on his vest. This inspector is always breathing down Ace's neck, as if he is always a suspect." (A reminder of how Homicide Inspector LeFevre, played by Jack Webb, always was breathing down the neck of Jeff Chandler, star of *Michael Shayne, Private Detective*, a popular radio crime series in the late 1940s. Isn't it amazing, I think, how a show of forty years ago still has its lasting impressions.)

As Conway describes it, Crawford, behaving as if he were Sam Spade, slips back into the waterfront fog at the end of each episode, on some occasions falling into an open manhole. Yet none of his friends, not even the timid accountant that often helps him solve the capers, played by Joe Regalbuto, knows where he comes from or where's he going back to.

Conway finally relaxes his entire body, as if he is no longer anybody but Tim Conway. "I guess you could say this dumb comedy is being played seriously."

CBS, which has been Conway's home network for a decade or more, asked him to develop a detective comedy show years ago, but instead he opted for variety formats. Recently, Conway worked in a play called *Wally's Café*, in which he ages to eighty-two as the proprietor of a desert restaurant. It was an important moment for Conway, after years of comedy roles that tended to fall into his lap. "This kind of play is a security bag for an old-timer like myself. Every once in a while, an actor has to pay a character with some depth, just so he knows he still has what it takes."

Conway struck up a friendship with the play's author, Ron Clark, and together they concocted a pilot show. "I liked Ron's techniques of writing and felt it was time I did something I hadn't been doing. I remembered what CBS had thought about me being a private eye. I decided I wanted to try this new approach."

Conway is no stranger to writing. He has scripted many of his own movies, often in a flurry of words and paper that lasts for very short periods. *The Prize Fighter* (1979) he claims to have written in less than forty-eight hours. Others include *They Went That-a-Way & That-a-Way* (1978), and the Sherlock Holmes parody, *The Private Eyes* (1980). In comparison, *Ace Crawford* was one he really labored over. "One episode took me three days."

Conway still considers himself basically a physical comedian who has always avoided political humor. "Racial jokes are out; so is foul language. In fact, anything that might divide an audience, I avoid like a plague. I go right down the middle."

Conway was born Thomas Daniel Conway in Willoughby, Ohio, just outside of Cleveland, in a condition that, he claims, is no different from the way he looks today. "I was bald and cherub." He further claims he never had any desires in those early days to be a comedian. "I never even used to put lampshades on my head during parties." Acting was the furthest thing from his mind. Little theater for $25 a week wasn't his idea of a career. Yet he was destined for a comedian's career. "I was in the wrong place at the right time."

The wrong place was KWY-TV in Cleveland, where he had gone after two years of service in the U.S. Army to write TV comedy promotional spots. He graduated to writing humor bits for morning host Ernie Anderson, and the two developed a partner relationship that grew in strength. Later, after moving to WJW (a CBS affiliate also in Cleveland), Anderson was elevated to portraying a horror host named Ghoulardi. He/it/the thing became a wildly popular character, with Conway often appearing in segments he had also created. Around this time, Conway changed his first name to Tim, to avoid confusion with film actor Tom Conway.

The turning point came when comedienne Rose Marie saw some of his TV bits with Ghoulardi and arranged for him to audition for *The Steve Allen Show*. They loved him in New York, but Conway still "scratched my head" and wondered what all the fuss was about.

He became a Steve Allen regular, doing comedic "man in the street" bits. Thus it was that the rotund, 5' 8" clown had found a favorable home with Americans who enjoyed his floundering, crumbling characters.

Then came the four-year role that insured his longevity: bumbling, always-confused Ensign Charlie Parker on *McHale's Navy*. After he docked from that, Conway was involved with the failed pilot of *Turn-On*, enjoyed moderate success (would you believe thirteen weeks?) with his own variety hour and sitcom (all in his own name). Then came a most more successful four-year stint on *The Carol Burnett Show* in comedy skits as The Old Man (aka Duane Toddleberry) and Mr. Tudball, who spoke with a bizarre Swedish accent.

"The world," says Conway, "was at my feet, and I kept wondering what I had done to deserve it." He acknowledges that "I was a comedian's comedian. Whatever I did, it came naturally. I didn't have to work at it. So things kept coming my way. People allowed me to do whatever was funny."

CBS gave the go-ahead for only five episodes of *Ace Crawford, Private Eye*. Ratings over the next month or so will determine if Ace ever comes back out of the fog after the fifth night. If Conway is wrong about the way Crawford should have been played, he may fall through that manhole and be devoured by sewer monsters, or topple over the side of that pier and drown. Does the public want Conway as the cocky, self-assured, tight-lipped fool, or as it knows him best—as the idiotic fumbler-bumbler?

"In this business," says Conway, winking, "it's not a case of sinking or swimming. It's a case of walking back out of the fog."

After those five episodes on CBS, Ace Crawford was never seen again, but it didn't make any difference to Conway. He has stayed busy ever since. Along the way, he was nominated for twelve Emmy Awards, winning five. He and Harvey Korman, his co-star on *The Carol Burnett Show*, got together to make a DVD of new comedy skits called *Together Again*. Conway has also starred in eight video shorts spoofing various sports as a character named Dorf. He continues to thrive and to be as funny as ever.

ERNIE ANDERSON
Keep Cool With the Ghoul
Ernie Anderson, One of the Best Horror Hosts

Remember Ghoulardi, the TV horror host with whom Conway had worked at that TV station in Cleveland? They even toured together with a comedy act before they both ended up in Hollywood. Anderson found his own niche as a promotional voice-over specialist at the ABC Network. Then, in March 1991, I had the opportunity to meet and talk to him about his horror character.

We met because of Joe Bob Briggs (real name: John Irving Bloom), whom I had first met when his syndicated *Dallas Times Herald* "Drive-In Movie" column appeared in the Sunday Datebook of *The San Francisco Chronicle*. In those days, we all called him Joe Bob and he reviewed low-budget genre films with his tongue firmly implanted in his cheek, i.e. your weekly drive-in movie critic with caustic, amusing comments about the worst of Hollywood. His critique would sum up the total number of dead bodies in a film, as well as the number of bare breasts that had popped up or the pints of blood spilled.

Back in the early 1980s, he had told me, "I'm a Texas redneck character, and I take on any genre of lousy movie, as long as it's cheap and crappy. Movies' mainstream critics look down their puffy noses at these as beneath contempt and therefore avoid them if they were Bubonic Plague. And because these movies were ignored, I felt I'd be the one to review them. See, Joe Bob evolved out of a love for movies. I chose a writing style that reflected the thinking of a Texan who'd see the grisliest film playing. Sleaze classics. Janet Maslin of *The New York Times* condemned these movies as too violent, but without ever seeing one of them. You had to go to drive-in theaters or 42nd Street in Manhattan to find them. In Texas, you went solely to the drive-in."

That's Ernie Anderson at the foot of the staircase at the Magic Castle in Hollywood. Towering above him, left to right: movie critic Joe Bob Briggs, yours truly, long-time horror host John Zacherle, and horror hostess Elvira, aka Cassandra Peterson. My one question to her that day: "Tell me, Elvira. What is it you have as horror host that I don't?"

During that tenure, Joe Bob contacted me and invited me to be one of four horror-hosts from the past who would be the featured guests on his shows. All four episodes were to be taped at the Magic Castle, a museum and performance center dedicated to the art of magic. Located in Hollywood, just two blocks from Hollywood Boulevard, the Magic Castle was a showcase for such magicians as David Copperfield and David Blaines, a bastion for legerdemain and card manipulations, and a museum for the memorabilia of such greats as Houdini and Howard Carter.

The foursome, whom Joe Bob considered "the best horror hosts of all time," included myself, Ernie Anderson (aka Ghoulardi), Cassandra Peterson (aka Elvira-Mistress of the Dark), and John Zacherle (sometimes spelled Zacherley). We all met in the Palace of Mystery, a theater where normally magicians and sleight-of-hand arts performed. Connected was a bar patterned after a seventeenth century London pub.

On that fate-filled day when we all came together, October 11, 1991, I had an opportunity to talk to Anderson, hoping he would stress his characterization of Ghoulardi.

"Look," he answers, "that all happened back in the early 1960s in Cleveland. Yes, the character was popular and I yocked it up talking like a beatnik character. I'd dress up in a laboratory coat, fright wig, goatee, and mustache. This idiotic image hit Cleveland like a tidal wave. Viewers all but gobbled it up. We used crazy music and I would often blow up small objects on the set. And Tim [Conway] was a Godsend with his clever writing."

By the summer of 1963, Ghoulardi had introduced his motto, "Keep Cool With the Ghoul." It was the motto of all Cleveland, if not all of Ohio. "I was receiving 4,000 letters a week. Postcards. Sweatshirts. I even started doing a second show, wrapping my gruesome comedy around Laurel and Hardy short subjects. I loved superimposing my face within the movie scenes and shouting 'It's awful, it's terrible" over the soundtrack." Other taglines he used were "What a Dog!" and "What a Bomb!"

"You have no idea how I hit that town," Ernie told me. Born in Lynn, Massachusettes, he served in the U.S. Navy during World War II, and afterwards worked at various East Coast radio stations as "a commonplace disc jockey," commonplace until he started slipping in novelty records that didn't go over so well with managements. It was only a tip of his sense of humor and gradually that sense of humor started to show more.

"With the creation of Ghoulardi, the world opened up at my feet and never closed again. 'All the world's a purple knif' became

Ghoulardi's catch-line, knif being fink spelled backward." Everybody in town was hep to 'knif' talk," says Anderson, and Time magazine wrote him up as an Ohio oddity, a Cleveland cut-up whose ghoulish antics were gobbled up and swallowed whole by consumers. But it only lasted until 1966.

Eventually, Anderson came West to join the ABC network as one of its announcers.

I have been told in advance that Ernie became instantly famous for his voice. Ask, I am told, about the TV series *The Love Boat*. I do.

He pauses, a wry smile working its way around the corners of his mouth before he allows three "little" words to roll languidly, lingeringly off his tongue: "THHHEEE . . . LOOOOVVVEEE . . . BBBOOOAAATTT."

Stretching out those words "has made me very rich. Those three words have made me so rich I can laugh at it all." He has become one of the highest-paid announcers in Hollywood thanks to that voice. "Yeah," he says, "voiceovers, commercials, that's where it finally was at for me. You want 'LOOOVVVEEE . . . BBBOOOAAATTT" . . . you get 'LOOOVVVEEE . . . BBBOOOAAATTT.' Why should I deprive you of hearing it again . . . 'LOOOVVVEEE . . . BBBOOOAAATTT.'"

I was amazed to learn that Ernie became the announcer for *The Carol Burnett Show*, the very showcase for his pal Tim Conway. What a strange coincidence both of them should end up on the same program. One on camera, the other invisible to the eye but wonderment to the ears. "That's when I began to develop a new style that set a new standard for network announcing. They called me 'The Golden Throat' after I did the TV specials *Winds of War* and *Roots* . . . and yes, 'LOOOVVVEEE . . . BBBOOOAAATTT." You see, my SSSHHHIIIPPP finally CCCAAAMMMEEE in."

Ernie Anderson died in 1997 at the age of seventy-three, but, and this gets macabre in a Ghoulardi sort of way, his voice isn't dead. You can buy online lines Ernie recorded years ago for a fee–tag lines once used for promotions. If he were alive, he would scream, "What a DDDOOOGGG!"

Long-entrenched horror hostess, Elvira, also known in some circles as Cassandra Peterson, was kind enough to send me this signed photograph, in response to my question about what qualities she had as a horror hosting star that I seemed to be lacking in.

GALE GORDON
The TV Comedian Who Still Has A Love Affair with Old-Time Radio

"But he's not entitled to a commalary . . . uh uh uh . . . to a salary . . . as a murderer . . . as a member of the common tonsil . . . uh town council . . . what I mean to say . . . the streets . . . he . . . she . . . we all . . . uh . . . that is . . . we . . . me . . . he . . . I . . . (long pause) McGEE, will you please walk down to Dugan's Lake and jump up and down on the ice REAL HARD!"

Mayor Latrivia never could maintain his composure in the presence of Fibber McGee and Molly, portrayed by the husband-wife team of Jim and Marian Jordan. Every time Latrivia entered that Wistful Vista residence, beginning in 1941, and the McGees attacked him or his Wistful Vista administration, the mayor would sputter, fume, and ultimately end up tongue-tied. For *The Fibber McGee and Molly Show*, it was always a classic moment, one that listeners had been anticipated from the moment he began his characterization.

The pause between the final sputter and the low-pitched, deliberate "McGEE" was one of the longest and most effective in radio's history of comedy shows, a pause that was surpassed only one time by Jack Benny's prolonged silence as he decided if he wanted to part with his money or his life.

Gale Gordon was a master of radio comedy voices. In fact, the medium's history is riddled with his vocal presence, first as the easily-flustered, blustering LaTrivia, then later on the same show as a weatherman named Foggy Williams. In the 1950s, he would become the blustery school principal, Osgood Conklin, on *Our Miss Brooks* opposite Eve Arden.

While some actors had trouble making the transition to television, Gordon's expressive face and plump body immediately carried him into the video version of *Our Miss Brooks*. Later, he worked with Dennis Day, Alan Young, and then Bob Sweeney in the 1956 sitcom, *The Brothers*. For the past few years, Gordon has

Gale Gordon, looking pretty much the way he did the day we had lunch overlooking the harbor of Sausalito.

been working exclusively with Lucille Ball. For a while, he was the tight-fisted banker Theodore J. Mooney on *The Lucy Show*. Now he is Uncle Harry (Lucy's brother-in-law) on *Here's Lucy*.

Gale Gordon

The Gordon profile hasn't changed much since the days of LaTrivia. He is still the rotund comedy figure, prone to explode at the slightest provocation, eternally harassed by a world that seems to go out of its way to make things complicatedly unpleasant. After all those years, LaTrivia/Conklin/Mooney remain on the brink of flipping out, eager to be committed to the nearest asylum—just to escape the rest of the crazy world.

Comes the moment we meet in late May 1973. His limousine pulls up to the curb in front of the San Francisco Chronicle building at Fifth and Mission, and I slide in. He's decided we are going to have lunch in Sausalito, a bayside community just a couple of miles past the northern end of the Golden Gate Bridge. As we move slowly through midday traffic, Gordon's voice is actually quite soft and melodic. His manner is quiet, almost meditative. He tends to gaze for long periods out the window as it makes its way across the Golden Gate Bridge. At least the tempo of life, or the memory of McGee, hasn't flustered or agitated the real Gale Gordon.

So he sits in the backseat, relaxing, smoking, talking, and then going silent while he seems to be giving some private matter deep thought. Always gentle. Always calm. LaTrivia, Conklin and Uncle Harry belong back on a sound stage in Hollywood.

Our luncheon destination is the Altamira Hotel in Sausalito. Although it's well past noon when we arrive, scores of people are still sunning and stuffing themselves on the second-floor outdoor patio. Gordon pauses to watch the sailboats sprinkled across the water, and gazes for a while at the spectacular view of San Francisco. Finally, he selects a table near the edge of the balcony and sits silently for a while, smoking a new cigarette and in no hurry about anything.

Finally, when the cigarette is about half gone, I ask him about being an actor. "I've never been a compulsive one," he says. "I'd rather be in overalls, in my workshop, building or fixing something. My wife, Virginia, and I live on a 150-acre spread near Borrego Springs, which means we get away from it all a lot and live in some solitude we both love." No matter that he has to drive 160 miles to get back to Los Angeles on any day of taping.

He removes his sunglasses to clear away a speck of lint from the lens. Sunlight glistens off a pin attached to the lapel of his dark suit that reads, "Pro Deo Rege Patria" (translation: "For God, King, and Country"). It's a memento of his education at Woodbridge School in Suffolk when he returned to England in 1921-1922 to complete his education. (Although born in New York, his parents soon took him to England, where he was reared for eight years.)

"You know," he says, dipping into a shrimp salad, "radio in those days was an easy life. You didn't have to memorize lines; you had the script right in your hand. All you had to do was get over microphone fright and turn the pages quietly. From then on, you were all right."

He recalls the days when he was getting $150 a week to do a single McGee show. Gordon's face is not the kind that lights up, but there is a certain tugging effect at the corners of his mouth which indicates an inner pleasure. "That was big money in those days for an unknown like myself."

There lingers within Gordon a great love for old-time radio, as evidenced by the thousands of tape collectors across the country. Gordon still has his own love affair going with radio and can sit for hours and talk about its progress and performers.

"Radio certainly had its advantages over TV. Listeners could mentally cast the shows to fit their own needs. When TV came along, that part of the imagination was put to sleep. In other cases, certain people didn't live up to expectations. That's why the Jordans (Fibber McGee and Molly) never made the transition. They saw their TV pilot and shelved the project."

Lucille Ball, claims Gordon, "is the kind of comedienne you learn something from every day, even after working with her for years. It's still a stimulating experience. She instantly knows what will or won't play. Instinctively. She's always right."

He then told me a fascinating footnote to TV history. "Lucy had originally wanted to hire me to play her next-door neighbor on *I Love Lucy*. But at the time, back in the early 1950s, I was contractually tied down to *Our Miss Brooks*, and had to refuse the part. Eventually, that next-door neighbor was played by Bill Frawley. Maybe you've heard of him. What I missed was the opportunity to play one of the most popular characters in the history of TV."

Even after lunch is over, neither of us are in a hurry to go anywhere. I keep up the questions about old-time radio and he talks about the actors and the programs, coming up with new memories about those good old days. Then, he falls silent, staring out over the waters of Sausalito, remembering, smoking, thinking....

Lucille Ball had wanted Gale Gordon to portray her next door neighbor on I Love Lucy, but he had other commitments, and admits that he missed an opportunity of a lifetime.

"I did not mind a briber . . . bribe a minor . . . when I stole the fur . . . I mean when the furman murpiece . . . the urman fur . . . to steal for us both . . . I wasn't . . . I can't . . . I . . . you . . . me . . . you . . . but . . . *McGEE!*"

Gordon would complete a total of 140 episodes of *Here's Lucy*, and later join Lucille Ball to do *Life With Lucy* in 1986. He would spend the rest of his life living on his ranch in Borrego Springs, dying in 1995 at the age of eighty-nine.

PHYLLIS DILLER
The Well-Shod Comedienne
Who Led Me Down the Hall
Into Her . . . Master Bedroom?

To enter the home of Phyllis Diller in September 1966 is to slip into a specialized realm of madness, but with a tone of hysterical laughter ringing in the background. The first indication of insanity is just a few feet inside the front door to her posh, two-story, English country-style manor located in suburbia Brentwood. It is a vertical painting which has been hung on the wall in a horizontal position.

I ask myself, *Should I stand on my head, or just spread myself onto the floor?*

The second sign of kookiness is Phyllis herself, who instantly appears in the hallway clad in a lacy, two-piece olive-green bellbottom lounging outfit, accented in singular fashion by suede high-heel shoes. Her hair, as usual, looks as though an eggbeater has just passed through it, and in my mind I hear a whirring noise, as if the eggbeater is still active and perhaps approaching my own head of hair. I scratch the top of my head to be sure. "Don't let that picture on the wall bother you," Phyllis nearly screeches in the wake of her initial greeting to me. "There's nowhere in the house it'll fit lengthways."

There are an additional twenty-two points of derangement that follow—each is a room in the Diller Domicile, a home first built in the 1920s by a money-burdened politician, Lawrence C. Phipps, one-time Senator from Colorado. A powder room near the main entrance is affectionately labeled Edith's Head, named after a famed Hollywood costume designer. The Doris Day Room, where Phyllis relaxes and does her reading, is made from "virgin wood."

We are not strangers to each other. I first met Phyllis at the Purple Onion, the subterranean nightclub in San Francisco's North Beach, where she had first been discovered back in 1955, and from where she bounced upward into a nonstop career of

Phyllis Diller, clad in hilarious female dress, always with the cigarette holder. This is the way I remember her from her early days performing at the Purple Onion, and the way she looked when I ventured to her home.

Is this Phyllis Diller trying her best, dress-wise, to look like a millionairess living in Southampton, New York, instead of the kooky babe of stand-up comedy?

sharp-tongued, self-deprecating comedy. On the night of that initial meeting, we were watching a new comedian perform. I heard a unique sound of laughter coming from behind me and knew instantly it had to be Phyllis. It was the way she laughed at herself when she performed. No other woman on earth laughed in that fashion. I took time to single her out after the show and explained my *San Francisco Chronicle* connection. We would meet off and on over the next few years, and so it was a natural that I should want to cover her very first breakthrough into television—a new ABC series called *The Pruitts of Southampton*.

As I stand in the hallway, reminding her of our various meetings, she begins to wiggle a finger at me and moves down the hallway, as if she wants me to follow her. "There's something I really want to show you," she says, emphasizing "really" as if it's something very close, very personal. There's even a touch of seductiveness in her voice, and I wonder what she "really" has in mind. She walks in an alluring manner into . . . I pause to catch my breath. We have entered her master bedroom and, continuing to wiggle her finger at me, we move in unison toward a large double bed. I pause, wondering . . . no, this isn't the Phyllis I know. But, once I'm next to the bed, she drops her finger back to normal, stops wavering her buttocks and looking seductive, and slides open a large closet door.

"I'm so proud of these," she proclaims, pointing to a collection of every kind of female shoe imaginable. "I love to collect shoes. High heels are the funnywear for my shows. It's a grand, undying fetish with me." Next, she reveals a long row of what she calls "zany dresses," as well as three coats made from striped skunk— "three flavors valued at $10,000."

An investigation of her home continues. She has six fireplaces, six pianos, and a total of seven bedrooms. Scattered through these rooms are numerous paintings and chairs, items Phyllis collects as someone might save stamps and coins. One compartment is crammed with nothing but musical instruments: xylophone, drums, trumpet, guitars, another—yikes!—piano! No big surprise since Phyllis plays piano, organ, and harpsichord. Early in her life, she wanted to be a musician, but soon gave it up when she decided that she didn't possess the talent to develop into a professional musician.

Finally, as though she has no more treasures to show me, she leads the way into a massive front room, commonly known as the

Phyllis Diller, a woman of pure energy, who could even make her hair look like it was standing on end.

Bob Hope Salon, where a butler, who speaks only a smattering of English, waits to serve a cocktail in polished Continental style. "The reporter who was here just before you," Phyllis explains, "spilled his booze on my $16,000 carpet, there at your feet. But don't let that bother you in the slightest. Drink or spill all you desire." And, oh yes, she adds, it's quite permissible to sit on the 1670 Cassone cabinet, now a museum piece, located next to the window.

Phyllis herself takes a davenport next to an oil portrait of Bob Hope, a cigarette encased in the long holder she grips in her thin fingers. She explains that Hope has been a mentor to her, and gave her the painting as a way of solidifying their friendship. She makes some comment about preparing veal scallopini for dinner guests, then bursts forth with her famous cackle.

I ask myself, somewhere beneath the inane clothing and the put-on professionalism of the comedienne, could there be a different Phyllis Diller, the onetime Mrs. Sherwood "Fang" Diller, who wrote bright, witty commercial copy for Bay Area radio stations, and who raised a family of five in Alameda before her entry into show biz? (By the way, "Fang" she will tell me, is a made up character and has nothing to do with her first husband, from whom she is now divorced, or the one who now lives with her in the home.

How does a reporter get to that woman? Or does that woman even exist anymore? Perhaps she has so submerged herself into the one-state Diller that the old, pre-show business personality has become lost, forgotten,

As the conversation wears on, and congeniality develops, a chasm suddenly presents itself in the Diller veneer. It isn't very big, and it is nearly concealed amidst all the clever barbs and cynical wisecracks: A touch of the starry-eyed girl is still alive, pulsating inside Phyllis.

For despite eleven years of fame and fortune in the best of supper clubs and nights spots as a leading lady of laughter, wearing fright wigs of various colors, smoking cigarettes in long holders, and delivering housewife self-hatred shtick loaded with guffaws, Phyllis still has a great flaming ambition, an almost naive desire in view of all her other successes and hardships.

Her goal is to be the star of her own weekly TV situation comedy series, which she has now achieved with *The Pruitts of Southampton.*

She has, in her own words, "finally arrived."

Phyllis blows smoke into Bob Hope's nose. "Honey, you won't believe this, so get your body ready for a big shock. Ever since I got my big break at the Purple Onion in San Francisco back in 1955, I've wanted my own TV show. Like nothing I've ever wanted before. I wanted a series wild and creative, something experimental.

And this is the big moment. I'm a hot body now," she says, followed by a fresh burst of cackles. "A real life property, get it?"

I am forced to remind Phyllis, "But the critics have received your show with lukewarm to ice-cold response."

"Listen, honey, Phyllis Pruitt is a character brimming with zest, and that's me—bubbling nonstop with zest, zest. The show is elegant drawing-room comedy, and the characters are near reality. I mean, Southampton is a real place, a chic hangout on Long Island. I play a millionairess who suddenly finds she doesn't have a dime but she's got to keep up the family facade. I'm down on my heels but I'm up on my toes. Good thing I have all of those shoes to wear.

"This is a spoof of the establishment, of the old social register set. You know, after fifteen years, the neighbors still don't speak to each other. Phyllis Pruitt has a little Auntie Mame in her. She's the type that gives the dog the leftover drink as a tranquilizer."

Phyllis' enthusiasm wanes a trifle (but not her wit) when she thinks back to the years she spent on the road, one booking after the other, with little time for personal considerations. "I needed the energy of an Olympic runner. Honey, I'd do one show, rush to my hotel room, spray under my arms, and rush out to do another show.

"I'd reached the point where I had to slow down a little. Let's face it, I'm forty-nine years old and I've never wasted a minute of my life. Now, with the TV series, I can start living like a normal human being. I mean, I've got this house now, and I can go to bed at a decent hour."

Phyllis leans back on the davenport, contentedly blowing out a ring of smoke. "Yes, for the first time I'm going to get a chance to enjoy this kooky, goofball world of mine."

Although her series was retitled *The Phyllis Diller Show* to improve its rating, it was cancelled at the end of just one season. Somehow she survived the loss and went on to live a fulfilled life working in movies, doing voice-overs and comedy appearances until her death in 2012 at the age of ninety-five. She died in the home where I interviewed her and saw her in person for the last time. Still surrounding her were all those musical instruments, which she had promised to me she would never give up.

Phyllis Diller during her days of starring on The Pruits of Southampton, *always shocked by the world around her.*

KEN CURTIS
Cutting Through the Gunsmoke —The Twangy Voice of Festus, Cantankerous But Loveable

In the beginning, singing cowboys weren't supposed to be funny, although it might sound rather silly today that a cowboy star, right in the middle of the action, would pause to sing a frontier melody. Just when the ranch is under attack from marauding Indians, or the heroine is screaming her lungs out for help as the villain reaches for her luscious body. But then, song over, the saddle hero swung back into action with blazing six-shooters. Gene Autry and Roy Rogers did it a lot, but so did some lesser-known cowboy stars, such as Ken Curtis.

Ken started out as a singer for the Tommy Dorsey Orchestra in 1941. By 1945, he was popular enough to be signed by Columbia to make a series of "musical Westerns" with the Hoover Hot Shots and a comedy sidekick played by Guinn "Big Boy" Williams. Surely you remember *Rhythm Round-Up* (1945), *Throw a Saddle on a Star* (1946), *Over the Santa Fe Trail* (1947), and . . . whoa, time to get back on the prairie.

What came next for Curtis, twern't nothin' comedic about it. He joined the Sons of the Pioneers, a popular band of drugstore cowboys, who struck pay dirt by singing songs that frequently became popular and were used in feature films. Without a doubt, there was never another Country and Western group quite like them hummin' hombres. From 1949-1952 Curtis was the group's lead singer and helped to make "Tumbling Tumbleweeds" and "Cool Water" memorable hits.

From there, Curtis became a strong supporting player in films, having through marriage become the son-in-law of director John Ford. He was featured in one John Wayne film after another—*Rio Grande* (1950), *The Quiet Man* (1952), *The Wings of Eagles* (1957), etc.

On this photo of Ken Curtis portraying his Gunsmoke character, Festus, he eagerly wrote, "For my friend John with a mess of sincere best wishes."

While he was appearing in *The Searchers* (1956) with John Wayne, he began clowning around with a twangy voice. Director Ford overheard that twang and insisted that Curtis use it for his part. It definitely turned a straightforward character, Charlie Mc-Corry, into something moviegoers would remember. Next thing he knew, Curtis was doing that same twang on an episode of *Have Gun-Will Travel* (1959) that went over so well he was brought back to do five more episodes.

Curtis, dropping the twang entirely, was chosen to play an adventurous parachutist, Jim Buckley, in the *Ripcord* series (1961-63). Then, the day came in 1959 when Dennis Weaver gave up his role as Chester Proudfoot on *Gunsmoke*, and CBS needed a new face in Dodge City.

That's when the character of Festus Haggin was introduced on *Gunsmoke* as a cantankerous, often-rude, often-silly jail custodian for Marshal Matt Dillon. In early 1973, I am given the opportunity to meet with Curtis, now considered a leading character-comedian.

> "Don't you listen to him, Dan,
> He's a Devil not a man,
> And he spreads the burning sand with water
> ... Cool ... clear ... water ...."

During a noisy luncheon hour in a North Hollywood restaurant, Ken Curtis is feeling feisty as he reminisces about "those good old days" singing with the Sons of the Pioneers. "Pat Brady, he passed away last year, but a lotta the fellas are still around, like Bob Nolan and Shug Fisher. Those were the best of times for all of us, singing and getting roles in John Ford's wonderful cavalry movies. *Rio Grande* (1950), *The Searchers* (1956)."

"And Festus?" I ask.

"Festus marks the culmination of everything I've always wished for as an actor," he replies. "I love the character of Festus, and not just because he's proven to be a goldmine. He's a delight, an actor's dream. He's one of a kind. He's got so many sides to him; he's tender, mean, warm, cantankerous, ornery, gentle, half outlaw, illiterate. All he's really got going is his animal cunning. If Festus doesn't like you, he can be on the sneaky side; on the other hand, if he likes you, he can be nice as hell. I call him a half-snaky deputy."

Jails and outlaws and colorful old characters were all part of Curtis' upbringing. "My dad was sheriff in Bent County, Colorado, for three terms. You won't believe this coincidence, but when I was only twelve, I helped him out as turnkey. And I helped mom cook for the prisoners. The jail was upstairs and we lived downstairs.

"That was in the days of a lot of desperate bank robber types. I remember we came close to a run-in with the Fleagle Gang, which was robbing banks by the score. Dad, he lived to be eighty-seven, training race horses right up to the day he died at the track—with his boots on. If you're gonna go, I guess that's the way to do it."

Curtis still remembers quite vividly the old character they called Cedar Jack. "Old Cedar, he'd provide logs for corrals. He'd disappear into the wilderness for about six weeks, load up with logs, and bring them to town. He'd always go on a big bender next thing, spend all his money, and wind up unshaven, broke and drunk. He wore this tall crown hat with no crimp. He was certainly in the back of my mind when I started creating the character of Festus."

Curtis spends about 190 days a year on the road doing rodeos, fairs, and other personal appearances. "I come on dressed as Festus, because people, hell, they don't give a hoot about Ken Curtis. They've come to see a character they can identify with.

"Underneath it all, I'm still a singer at heart, so it throws them a little when I drop the dialect and do pop and Western songs. Familiar tunes. When you're working in large arenas before 10,000, 20,000 people, you've got to give them something they know. Milburn Stone, he's Doc, he used to go with me on these tours, but since his heart attack, he doesn't go as often. Isn't quite the same what it used to be without him."

He tells me he has no intention of leaving *Gunsmoke* for any reason. "I'd be a fool not to reap the harvest. On the other hand, when CBS gives up the show, I think I'd leave the film and TV business. I'd like to raise horses, maybe tend to some cows, take care of some chickens. I love the high country around Sante Fe, New Mexico. Get me a ranch there and settle down. About the only place left where I'd be happy. It's out there in that emptiness where a man can still feel like there's still a little of God's country left after all."

> "Now Dan can't you see
> By that big green tree,
> The water's running free
> And it's waiting there for you and me.
> Cool ... clear ... water ...."

Reckon Ken Curtis turned up mighty lucky, playing Festus. He totaled up 304 episodes over an eleven-year period. After *Gunsmoke* folded in 1976, he moved on to do several TV Westerns, as well as a modern-day "soap opera Western," *The Yellow Rose* (1983-1984), in which he appeared in twenty-two episodes. He died in 1991 at the age of seventy-four of a heart attack. A most colorful career was over.

DOM DELUISE
Mr. Show Biz With All The Trimmings of Old King Cole

Most critics have been calling *The Twelve Chairs* a cinematic disaster, but you'd never guess it from the bouncing step and bubbly carbonation of Dom DeLuise. He sweeps into Bardelli's Restaurant in December 1970 to join me for dinner. *Wow, I think to myself, this portly spokesman with the rotund face is dropping cheery smiles on everyone in sight, and his one-liners zinging so fast they almost collide with waiters balancing silver trays of food.*

DeLuise's pose has the pseudo-grandeur of Dominique the Great, that recurring magician in his comedy sketches. He also sits at the table with all the attributes of Old King Cole, ready to ho-ho-ho his way through a plate of cracked crab.

DeLuise has come to San Francisco to promote Mel Brooks' new comedy, *The Twelve Chairs*, because he's one of the leading players as Father Fyodor, a Russian orthodox village priest who chucks the cloth to seek, in unrestrained fashion, a fortune in jewels that is hidden away inside one of twelve chairs. Abetting him in this "period caper" is an impoverished aristocrat (Ron Moody) and a con artist (Frank Langella).

However, DeLuise transcends anything as mundane as well-here-I-am-to-sell-a-flick. Instead, he becomes the Court Jester larger than life, wherein the whole world is a stage and every face is a camera focusing a wide-angle lens on him. Yes, folks, Dom DeLuise is Mr. Show Biz, that loveable entertainer who's in perpetual motion (mouth and hands, especially). With him on the set of real life, *The Twelve Chairs* seems as relevant and timely as the Cenozoic Era.

Even eating becomes a focal point of comedic action, as DeLuise flies into his plate of cracked crab, sucking out stringy morsels here, splitting away a shell there, and keeping everyone, including an uncertain waiter, entertained. "Am I allowed to do this with my fingers?" he asks, glancing at everyone seated at the table.

During our dinner, Dom DeLuise signed this photo. On the left: "John - It was good to talk to you—soon again, ok?" On the right: "Stay Happy - Dom DeLuise."

His hunger seems justified by the fact that he has undergone about twenty interviews during this single day . . . and hasn't it been a couple of hours since he last ate? DeLuise only stops short of sucking away the layer of ice covering his plate.

Peering over the heap of shells, the comedian/actor relates how insane Mel Brooks is. "An insane man, utterly crazy. But in a sweet, friendly way. That's why he's such a loveable guy . . . Please, take that garlic bread away. Don't tempt me with it. I'm not even allowed to breathe the fragrant aroma. I must suppress my desires. Yes, we spent six months in Yugoslavia. Yugoslavia, that's the opposite of San Francisco. The country has no color. Once there was a boy in a green shirt and they took him away. Nothing happened on weekends because Toto has the car. Glenn Ford films are big in Yugoslavia. The people laugh and scream every time Ford shoots someone.

"Peter Sellers was supposed to do the part of Fyodor, but he had to make *There's a Girl in My Soup* instead. I love that man for not being in two places at once. Thank God I exist, otherwise I wouldn't have landed the part. This priest, I play him straight at first, then I go raving bananas. Russia, 1927. No cookies, everyone's starving. Brooks, a twisted maniac. Crazy, like I said. He couldn't yell at himself as an actor because he's the director, too. Nuts, the man is nuts. That's why I love him."

All that has been said in a single breath.

What about *The Dean Martin Show*, which has done a great deal to propel DeLuise's career over the past three years?

"Ah, I still do ten segments a year, under contract. I entertain Dean. If he laughs, I know I'm doing all right. At first I did only set routines, then one night I broke my magic wand during my magic act and the audience roared. It taught me the value of the spontaneous action, and now Dean and I'll ad lib entire skits. Once we went for twelve minutes. TV is a spontaneous thing—football, fires, war. It's when it gets predictable that it's a drag. Can't those guys please take away that damn garlic bread?"

In a unique moment of solemnity, DeLuise admits that his own summer replacement series of 1968, taped in Miami, was not everything he had hoped. "With Dean, I could select my material and prepare, but in Miami I was faced with numerous sketches and little time to get ready. And they kept me on too long. I told them to get other acts, but they wanted me, me, me. Even for the best of talent it's tough to carry an hour-long show." DeLuise sniffs a piece of garlic bread, then repugnantly pulls back. "No, I mustn't. I mustn't. Doom hangs over me."

While DeLuise has found greatest recognition as a TV comedian (people tend to remember his one-man routines, especially the dentist office bit), he prefers to think of himself as a dramatic

Dom DeLuise also signed this photo to my son: "To Russ - Keep smiling and that's me on the bottom. On top, that's Bertha, a famous performer at the Nugget Casino in Sparks, East Reno."

actor who's occasionally clowning around. "Serious acting—that's what I want to do."

His first film was certainly serious. He played a traitor in *Fail-Safe* (1964). He was also kind of a gas in Mel Brooks' *The Producers* (1967), *The Glass-Bottom Boat* (1966), and *T. R. Baskin*, in which he portrays a lonely traveling salesman who spends a great deal of time in the nude with Candy Bergen. (Apparently, his scenes were cut from the film, as he is not listed in the final credits.)

Dom DeLuise in his role as Aunt Katherine "Kate" Abbot in the Gene Wilder-directed supernatural comedy, Haunted Honeymoon.

DeLuise credits the early TV comedians—especially Sid Caesar and Jackie Gleason—for influencing his style, but not Bob Hope, and definitely not Abbott and Costello. He enjoys Laurel and Hardy comedies (in fact, he is a buff of silent films) and often, he claims, he and his wife dress up to act out the comedy team's oldest routines. (For a few minutes, DeLuise imitates smashing eggs in his pocket and under his belt, imitating Oliver Hardy.)

Yes, life can be a gas when you're Dom DeLuise, but all is not rosy, as he points out. Take a recent elevator ride he had in Cleveland. "This drunken man, bless his soul, pinched me on the cheek, slapped me on the back, and introduced me to everyone else on the elevator as Jonathan Winters. What can you do? And this guy wouldn't let go of my hand the whole time. I had to go three floors beyond my stop."

A few minutes later, DeLuise says he has to leave for the Stage Door, where *Twelve Chairs* is having its premiere tonight. As he goes out the door, he's still grinning into those wide-angle lenses, and the waiters are still ducking the one-liners.

"Whew," says one of the old timers as the front door of Bardelli's slams shut.

Dom DeLuise would continue to work for Mel Brooks in such comedy classics as *Blazing Saddles* (1974), *Silent Movie* (1976), and

Spaceballs (1987), among many. He also became close to Gene Wilder and appeared with Wilder in *The Adventures of Sherlock Holmes' Smarter Brother* (1975) and in the Wilder-directed *Haunted Honeymoon* (1986). By 2008, he was suffering heavily from diabetes and high blood pressure. He then developed cancer and died in 2009 at the age of seventy-five.

JERRY COLONNA
Bob Hope's Second Banana Appealed As a Master of Visual and Vocal Comedy

The bulging eyes, the ticklish-looking mustache, and the high-pitched voice all add up to one comedian of long standing: Jerry Colonna. Call him Bob Hope's "Second Banana," since he was a co-star on Hope's radio show for a decade after being discovered on Bing Crosby's *Kraft Music Hall* when he did comedy with John Scott Trotter's Orchestra. Singing, or caterwauling, has also been part of his comedy.

Jerry Colonna, always a visual delight.

"I've devoted much of my life to show business," he tells me one night in the summer of 1961 during a break after one of his shows in Harrah's Lounge, a late-night venue at Harrah's Tahoe. "In fact, I gave up my San Fernando Valley home so I could spend more time entertaining troops abroad with my old buddy Bob Hope, or hanging out in Vegas or here near the Lake. I've discovered a new generation of fans (many of them youngsters) who have seen my old motion pictures on TV. Especially the Road Pictures I did with Bob and Bing: *Road to Singapore* (1940), *Road to Rio* (1947), and *Road to Hong Kong* (1962). They respond with very enthusiastic fan mail.

"This thing called show business is a lot of work," Colonna says. "It's difficult to always know what people think is funny. This is what I have to find out. If a comedian is naturally inclined he'll get the laughs. Actual joke telling is tough; you've got to find material to fit your own character.

"Voices," he says, "I love to do voices. I was the March Hare in Disney's *Alice in Wonderland* (1951) and I did the voice for the cartoon, *Casey at the Bat* (1946). I also did this thing 'Who's Yehoodi?' on Bob's show, and later in a 1943 cartoon version.

"You know, a lot of people have asked me why I don't tell jokes on stage, like I did on radio back in the old days. What they don't understand is that on Bob Hope's old Pepsodent radio show, we told imaginative situation comedy jokes. If we told a gag, for example, about some guy building a bridge on the Mississippi River lengthways, people could picture it. It was wild and zany. I never told a real joke on Bob's show."

Have all these years been a strain? "No," he says, "I still get satisfaction out of my work. Our act isn't too confining, and although we have a routine, it's flexible and we can give it an ad lib feeling. If I want to clown down to the front row I can; it keeps the tension from building up inside. Working here in Harrah's Lounge is more rewarding for me than if I was to do a show with an unvaried, straight format."

Five years after our meeting, Jerry Colonna suffered a stroke from which he never could fully recover. A heart attack in 1979 took him for the rest of his life to the Motion Picture and Television Hospital in Beverly Hills, where he died in 1986. When I interviewed Bob Hope in 1993, he told me that during the last months of the comedian's life he paid him a visit every day to keep him entertained. Colonna had been the most dedicated and beloved of all of Hope's friends.

Jerry Colonna with Bob Hope during their time as radio stars.

BARBARA EDEN
The Genie With an Ordinary Navel That NBC Tried to Hide

Up on the 16th floor of the Fairmont Hotel atop Nob Hill, overlooking the city of San Francisco, Barbara Eden is brushing her hair in the early hours of the morning.

Wearing her short-short-short nightie. I mean, the one that's very very very short.

She just happens to glance up, and there, hanging outside the window, are two men. They are frozen in place, gaping at her, just as she is now frozen into place, gaping at them. These men are professional window-washers, unconcerned at that moment about the art of cleaning panes high atop a hotel. Suddenly, they both come alive when they realize that Barbara is staring as hard at them as they are at her, and they begin lowering the ropes that are keeping them from plunging to the street below. Meanwhile, a window shade comes slamming down after Barbara has rushed across the room, even though she is still wearing her short-short-short nightie.

A short time later, Barbara is enjoying breakfast in the Camellia Room of the hotel, unfazed by the men-in-the-window incident. Staring males should hardly be anything new whether in her TV or real life, especially when you consider those skimpy costumes she wears and all that cheesecake that is being displayed to promote her as the beautiful-woman-in-a-bottle on *I Dream of Jeannie*, the NBC comedy gracing the airways on Monday nights. In March 1969, the series in now in its fourth season.

"Cheesecake?" queries Barbara, looking genuinely puzzled. "I wasn't aware of much cheesecake." Well, there was this rather busty picture in a popular tabloid, with her spilling out of her harem costume. She just shrugs it off.

Barbara, does it bother you being something of a sex image in the current Hollywood milieu?

"I don't mind."

Barbara Eden clad in her I Dream of Jeannie *costume, at least the costume that allowed her navel to be shown. Notice that Jeannie signed it, too.*

What about that silly business when NBC would not permit her to wear a certain costume that revealed her navel, the one located just beneath that flimsy piece of material atop her chest?

She giggles slightly.

(Note: There have been some photos taken of her with her navel showing, and there would seem to be nothing out of the ordinary about it. Just a good clean belly button. Wasn't all that business silly?)

Once again, Barbara Eden's navel is showing even better than on the previous page, given the designer dropped her lower apparel quite a bit more than previously. Aren't designers wonderful?

Giggle again.

What about staring men in general?"

"Don't they all?" Another giggle.

In the Camellia Room, there are male diners staring. Barbara has chosen a high-neck dress this morning, but it conceals nothing of her trim figure. Her blonde hair falls around her shoulders in the manner we have come to expect of movieland sexpots. In her case, there remains a degree of naiveté and wholesomeness. Her features have a tendency to appear childlike in the context of certain expressions, and her laugh is frequent and frothy with giggles.

What about all those years spent in that land of tragedy, Hollywood?

"Tragedy? I don't think there's anything tragic about Hollywood. It's only tragic if you choose to make it so. I've found nothing but happiness here. A career, a husband, a son. All a girl could ask for."

Originally, that girl was Barbara Huffman, who attended Lincoln High School of San Francisco at the same time Carol Channing was going there. In 1951, Barbara was crowned Miss San Francisco, a fact she doesn't like to discuss much, since it tends to have an aging effect. Being crowned wasn't what got her into the movies. If anything, a Miss San Francisco is exactly what Hollywood didn't want in the early 1950s, or at least it didn't want Barbara.

She came back to her home in the Sunset District and worked at a Wells Fargo bank, baby-sitting on the side to pay for spare-time singing lessons at the San Francisco Conservatory of Music and dramatic acting lessons at the Elizabeth Holloway School of Theater.

When she went back to Hollywood, she crashed the studio gates. The lessons hadn't exactly qualified her for the role of Lady Macbeth, but she did get the part of the dumb blonde in the TV version of *How to Marry a Millionaire*, a syndicated series (1957-1959) in which she was a ditzy model named Loco Jones.

Furthermore, she enjoyed subsequent dumb blonde roles in such fare as *All Hands on Deck* (1961), *The Brass Bottle* (1964), and *A Private's Affair* (1959). She feels they were unimportant roles, one and all, and when she appeared with her actor-husband Michael Ansara (whom she had married in 1958) in *Voyage to the Bottom of the Sea* (1961), she felt she might never resurface. When she appeared in *Five Weeks in a Balloon* in 1962 with producer-director Irwin Allen, she felt she would never touch dry land again.

She underestimated the importance of her role in *The Brass Bottle*, which featured Burl Ives as a genie and Tony Randall as the new master. Ironically, Barbara had simply portrayed another beautiful woman in the cast, for it was that role that had impressed Sidney Sheldon to think of her as the genie who pops out of a bottle.

In the beginning, she felt that a dumb blonde genie, granting her master Larry Hagman (portraying an astronaut, Major Anthony Nelson) his every wish (at least the kind that could be depicted on television in these days), was just another clichéd role. A spray of mist from a magical bottle, however, faired okay in the ratings, and today she is a major TV star.

Not even Barbara, however, can exactly tell you why. "TV," she tells me, "is like a game of roulette. You're taking just as much a chance when you bring together a writer, an actor, and a director. Sometimes the ball falls on your number. Sometimes it hits Double 00. Triple 000. I've been around long enough to be both a winner and a loser, and so I can only say that with the role of Jeannie I'm finally winning."

Whether Barbara expects *I Dream of Jeannie* to lead to more important roles, and perhaps elevate her out of the fluff category, she seems unequipped to say. "Drama, mystery, comedy—I don't know what I'd want." Maybe she just hasn't thought that much about it. Or perhaps her ambitions lie more toward being a mother and wife, since she glows with maternal pride and speaks excitedly about her four-year-old son, Matthew, and husband, Ansara.

Evidence of her love for show business is apparent, too, when she explains that although she failed with her nightclub act last summer in Las Vegas, she intends to return in the summer for another try. "This time," she vows, "there'll be less gimmicks and more of me. Me. A one-woman musical revue."

Meanwhile, for those who don't take in Las Vegas one-woman musical revues, there is still *I Dream of Jeannie*, which returns for its fifth season in September. It's nothing to laugh at, but when it comes to looking, it's super-filled with Barbara Eden.

The marriage to Michael Ansara will last until 1974. Tragedy will strike when her son Matthew dies of a drug overdose in 2001. The fifth season for *I Dream of Jeannie* was the last for the series as the ratings collapsed, but her acting career continued to be successful and she succeeded as a nightclub entertainer in Las Vegas and other cities.

GEORGE CARLIN
Here He Is, the One and Only Hippy Dippy Weatherman

In the late months of 1968, George Carlin was still struggling to find the best form of humor that was within him. He would go on to become one of the most controversial of comedians with his use of foul language, but in a context that tried to explain the dark side of man. Notice that he hints that comedy of the 1960s needed to be refreshed and updated, and he became just the comedian to do it.

Now, here he is, the world's only weatherman that doesn't work with a full deck, Al Sleet, your Hippy Dippy Weatherman.

Crackle! Fizzle! Sput Sput!

The static on the long-distance wire out of Los Angeles abruptly cuts off the nasal voice that just filled my unprepared ear. Then, after a short pause, the normal resonance of George Carlin comes into my ear a little more gently, with enthusiastic telephone amenities thrown in.

"Hear me loud and clear?"

I reply, "Roger!"

"No," says Carlin. "My name is George. George Carlin." *Nice beginning for an interview with a comedian,* I think, and get to the business at hand.

"Hey, George, that Al Sleet guy you created is a nutty one."

"A shtick is a shtick. A schmuck is a schmuck."

"So is that disc jockey you do who says 'Wonderful WINO!' Where'd you get the idea of satirizing the broadcasting world like that?"

"Today, everybody is in a broadcasting frame of reference. Al Sleet is the same guy you just saw last night on the eight o'clock news. Or take any disc jockey playing the Top 40. My idea is that they're all idiots. Communications is a great target for comedians—can you think of anything more vulnerable than TV commercials or a DJ plugging the Top 40? Then, don't forget, I spent

George Carlin, as he looked around the time I interviewed him in the 1960s.

three years in the U.S. Air Force winging it as a disc jockey. So, the whole thing is a distant but not forgotten part of me."

"Weren't you the partner of Jack Burns (now of Burns and Schrieber) back in the early 1960s?"

"Yeah, but we split up around March of '62 and I've been a single ever since. Done a lot of TV. First about twenty Merv Griffin shows. Then a whole summer with Buddy Greco as the replacement for Jackie Gleason. It's been a busy time."

"Can we expect to see anything new when you appear at Bimbo's 365 Club this coming Thursday night?"

"You bet. I'm reclaiming the kind of presentation I did before I got on TV, when I used to do nightclubs. I call it The Valley. It's a spot in the middle of pre-rehearsed bits wherein I slow down and ad lib bits and pieces. Four seconds at the most for any given gag. The Miscellaneous Bag."

"You've been making a lot of TV guest appearances on Ed Sullivan, Johnny Carson, Jackie Gleason. What do you feel is your chief asset as a comic, the single most appealing face that has put you in demand?"

"I listen well. I hear accents, content, small talk, lies, shallowness, giant stature. I hear everything I need to know for my material. Then I re-project these things with my own style added."

"Okay, but nobody is perfect. What about your weaknesses?"

"Although I find I invent very well in spontaneous situations, I find it hard to let myself go as much as I would like to. I need to be able to make that audience relaxed so it's not expecting an opera and I'm not afraid to take a chance with some untried material. Getting that feeling back in my gourd, that's largely my hang up."

"What comedians have you studied and admired, and which in some way reflect your own sense of humor?"

"Lenny Bruce got me started in the business. He was a friend, though I can't say a close friend. We'd get together whenever he was in town and he naturally inspired a lot of my ideas. Ohh . . . Jonathan Winters, W. C. Fields, Don Rickles, Lord Buckley, Mort Sahl. People like that."

"Who, in your opinion, are the up-and-coming?"

"Certainly Pat Paulsen. The Rowan and Martin *Laugh-In* troupe. Several of them will be heard from. Though none are now working in the traditional framework of comedy. They might even create a new kind of comic personality, a whole new fashion like the Second City or Committee. That school."

"Are you planning to move into other areas, broadening what so far has been only TV and nightclub exposure?"

"I just finished my first picture, *With Six You Get Egg Roll*, a thing with Doris Day and Brian Keith. I play a carhop in a drive-in. A dying breed, especially if you're a male."

"Is that good or bad, a Doris Day picture?"

"A part is a part, a part is a start."

"Are there any trends in comedy which you feel are tending in wrong directions?"

"One of the things holding back comedy today is a continuing preference for certain old-timers. I wouldn't mention any names because all are giants and have done well with what they work with. But I don't think they relate to today. It's an old bag and it breeds unawareness of what is currently happening."

"Is there anything you would like to add?"

"This is Al Sleet signing off, reminding you . . . I'm here only for the hail of it."

Where George Carlin was in 1968, when we talked, was nowhere compared to where he was going. His sense that most of the popular comedians of that period were behind the times was proven true, as Carlin moved away from the old-fashioned styles to establish a new one of his own in the 1970s, as did such comedians as Lenny Bruce, Shelley Berman, and others. Carlin became "the dean of counter-culture comedy," and became famous for using "seven dirty words," utter filth in the eyes of many. I found that out the hard way back in 2011, when I prepared a class for Bay Area Classic Learning based on the Top 20 Comedians as selected by Comedy Central. Carlin was positioned as #2 two among the Top 100 comedians. I warned my boss, David Kleinberg, that some of the seniors would object to the counter-culture approach Carlin always took. They didn't want to hear those seven dirty words, plus a few others. David told me to spare nothing when it came to Carlin. When I did the program, a couple of dames got up and walked out while I was playing my George Carlin segment. A call from Bay Area Classic Learning shortly afterward informed me that the class, because of those who walked out, was "a failure" and I wouldn't be doing it again any time soon.

Carlin suffered heart attacks off and on throughout the 1970s and 1980s, and finally succumbed to a final attack in 2008 at the age of seventy-one. After his death, he was awarded with the Mark Twain Prize for American Humor.

FRANK FONTAINE
Crazy Guggenheim Became Melodic – It Happened One Night Within the Soul of a Loveable Clown

The pudgy arm-waving figure on the stage of Bimbo's 365 Club, a popular nightclub in San Francisco's North Beach, is none other than Crazy Guggenheim, purveyor of the meatball gags (some funny, some less so, but all predicated on the lowest denominator, the pun), possessor of a discordant, moron voice, and the always-half-gassed confidant of Joe the Bartender on *The Jackie Gleason Show*. He's been doing that kind of outlandish comedy weekly since 1962, and now, it being the spring of 1966, he's here to carry out the Goofball Fontaine Style. Or is he?

For suddenly, a trio of scantily dressed cuties moves into the spotlight. One girl takes off his pink tie and replaces it with a flat bow tie; the second turns his checkered jacket inside out and it becomes a tuxedo; and the third removes the battered hat from his head.

The figure on stage is now Frank Fontaine, transformed into a warm, straightforward singer of popular, sentimental songs, some from the Tin Pan Alley era. So far, Fontaine has cut five albums for ABC-Paramount. The first one (*Songs I Sing on the Jackie Gleason Show*) sold so well it resulted in a Golden Album. Here he is, a weekly TV comedy actor, establishing a new image for himself. Will it confuse the public, or will he simply expand into new areas of entertainment? Backstage after his performance, I probe for an answer.

"All of a sudden," he says, "you fall into a groove of people who like your type of songs. You find yourself with a whole new following." There is something infectiously friendly about Fontaine. "My dad, Ray," he volunteers, "he was a strong man in a circus along with mom, an acrobat, and he had a voice like Mario Lanza. He'd say to me, 'Sing, Frank, sing.' I'd go, "Uhuhuhuhuhuhu, choke.' He'd just wince. But that wonderful guy made a good living off

Frank Fontaine and Jackie Gleason in a Joe the Bartender comedy sketch on Gleason's one-hour show during the 1960s.

his voice. So I kept trying to sing like my dad, but it came out . . . well, forget it. Sinatra would say, 'Hold it down, bud!' Tony Martin would say, 'Please, will ya leave town?' Tony Bennett would say, 'No, no, naughty boy.'"

Then, a few years ago, Fontaine took singing lessons and, "incredibly, I couldn't believe it myself," out popped a deep melodic voice. "I said to myself, *That's beautiful. But can I do it again? Was it an accident? A fluky moment?* Fontaine remembers turning to his instructor, who replied, "Do it always!"

From the beginning on the Gleason TV show, Fontaine was stuck with the Crazy Guggenheim character. "I told Jackie I wanted to do some other bits. I was a little disappointed with things. Jackie said, 'You're crazy. The viewers love Guggenheim. You gotta give the people what they want.' A year passed and I tried again. Jackie said, 'No, pal. Listen to me, pal. You can't change anything, pal. When the public loves you, you give 'em what they want. Get it, pal?' Of course, I had to listen. Jackie is the boss."

Then one evening, recalls Fontaine, he was in his dressing room singing ("I don't know why I love ya like I do . . . ") when Gleason and his manager, who were in a nearby room pondering over what singer to sign up for the next week's show, overheard his lyrics. Thus was Fontaine "discovered" all over again. Soon after, he introduced the singing into his act, surprising all who had been previously subjected to his Guggenheim role.

Fontaine, now forty-five, was born and raised in Cambridge, Massachusetts, and played in amateur shows when he was fifteen, doing impressions, pantomime bits, and telling stories. "I was also fifteen, when I invented Guggenheim. I was sitting on my aunt's porch and a bunch of kids, aged seven or eight, were fighting in the street. So I made them all cool off and sit down. I put on my baseball cap and started telling them the story of Little Red Riding Hood, talking in a crazy voice and mixing the fairy tale all up. Next day, there were forty kids in front of my house. 'Come out and tell us that story,' one of them shouted. The next day, there were even more kids showing up!"

The Guggenheim character would first become popular in 1950 on Jack Benny's radio show when, in response to Fontaine's request for a dime for a cup of coffee, Benny stepped totally out of character to give him a 50¢ piece because that was all he had in coinage. So it was that John L. C. Silvoney became a recurring character on Benny's radio and TV shows. Around this period, he landed comic roles in Frank Capra's *Here Comes the Groom* (1951) and *Call Me Mister* (1951).

Married, he became a dedicated father, as he co-created one baby after the other, deciding to give up after the eleventh was delivered. With such a growing family, Fontaine turned down film offers, following a policy of spending two weeks on the road, then staying home two weeks in Boston so he could get to know his children.

Fontaine, after four seasons with Gleason, will not be returning in the fall. "Jackie said he wasn't coming back, so I accepted other commitments. Then, CBS talked Jackie into doing another year, which left me out of the picture entirely. So, it's goodbye, Jackie. It was great while it lasted. Where do I go from here? Lots of singing, I hope, but who knows? I once did a comedy character I

Nobody could roll his eyeballs to look like a complete idiot better than Frank Fontaine, which made him stand out during his comedy career.

called Fred Frump, and Fred's dad once told him, 'You can never tell the depth of the well by the handle of the pump.' I'll just keep pumping along as best I can."

One would think Frank Fontaine would have had a great career ahead of him, but he had only ten years left to live. He guest starred one more time on Gleason's show and had a featured role in the 1973 film, *The Godmothers*. He died in Spokane, Washington in 1978, all of fifty-eight years old.

CLORIS LEACHMAN
Cloris Goes Bananas in Mexico, Then Takes a Walk Across My *Creature Features* Horror Set

When Cloris Leachman decides to stop being a sensible, normal person, brace yourself for the outrageous. What you might get is Frau Blucher of *Young Frankenstein* (1974), delivering such pearls of wisdom as "Stay close to the candles, the staircase can be treacherous" as she ushers you ever deeper into the inner sanctum of Mel Brooks' Gothic castle. Or what you might get is Nurse Diesel of the Psycho-Neurotic Institute for the Very, Very Nervous in Brooks' *High Anxiety* (1977), warning her very, very nervous patients that unless they are at the dinner table precisely at eight, "you will not get fruit cup."

Or what you might get is Louise, the Auntie Mame character with joie de vivre and a keen eye for a good-looking man in the Walt Disney comedy *This Goes Bananas* (1980). Herbie is the fourth film in the *Love Bug* series from Buena Vista—the three previous films reportedly grossed $200 million worldwide: *The Love Bug* (1969), *Herbie Rides Again* (1974), and *Herbie Goes to Monte Carlo* (1977). Herbie was an ordinary looking VW bug endowed with a thinking man's engine that becomes involved in the affairs of man. In the case of *Herbie Goes Bananas*, the civic-minded bug breaks up a ring of counterfeiters and rescues a kidnapped youth. Herbie's antics, such as fighting matador-style in a Tijuana bullring, have continually challenged the Disney special effects department.

When I meet Cloris as she swings through the Bay Area on a promotion tour in August 1980, she is obviously feeling her usual wild oats, serious one moment, zany as hell the next. She is so totally uninhibited and unpredictable that I don't know whether to ask serious or zany questions, so I try both. Sometimes she pooh-poohs the serious ones and seriously answers the zany ones. Her

The publicity photo Cloris Leachman signed to me and my wife Erica. It is barely readable today, but she scrawled, "Love, heh heh heh."

creative imagination, though, is always at work, reminding me they gave her an Oscar in 1972 for *The Last Picture Show* and Emmy Awards on four separate occasions for her work on *The Mary Tyler Moore Show* (1974), on *Cher* (1975), and in a TV movie, *A Brand New Life* (1973).

Cloris, whose hair is cut so short she compares herself to Mia Farrow, describes (with considerable delight) the great time she had making the latest Herbie flick. "Puerto Vallarta, one of the great resorts of the world, with those rugged rocky cliffs covered with vegetation. And they were paying us. Can you imagine it? Then, Guadalajara, my favorite Mexican city. We also went to Panama to do the scene where Harvey Korman (who plays Captain Blyth) glides his pleasure cruiser through the canal. You see, Herbie's been stored in the hole all this time, and there's a youth being held hostage, and . . . ."

I convince Cloris not to give away anymore of the plot and ask if she and Korman hadn't been diabolically teamed after their success together as the crazy nurse and the mad psychiatrist in Mel Brooks' *High Anxiety*?

"I supposed," she responds, "when two people create some funny business that comes off successfully, it's a natural inclination for a producer to take advantage of that, to see if there's some territory still unexplored. There's more fun to be had if two people can connect to make a joke work. Yes, Disney would be missing a good thing to deny us that opportunity."

Did it bother her, playing second banana to a battered VW?

"Second banana? Is that supposed to be a joke, son? Second banana is a Vaudeville term referring to a straight man, and I've played my share of straight men, but I never once felt I was playing second banana to an automobile. In fact, I've never felt I was second to anything. Or first to anything, for that matter. I just don't think that way—who is high or low. We take turns in life being high or low. It doesn't mean that someone is the best or less good. I just don't think that way."

I ask Cloris to describe herself.

She quickly replies, "I'm patient, allowing, intuitive about people, I have a sense of humor about myself. I was brought up not to expect a lot. I was brought up in Iowa country, during the Depression, on sunshine and orange juice." Cloris' father owned the Leachman Lumber Corporation. A good year was $6,000 gross. "At 4 a.m., I was washing clothes down in the basement. I hated to see anything caged and I'd even let the mice out of the wall. We had one acre of ground with a pasture and fishpond in the back. I'd fetch two buckets of water every morning. I remember the day that Jean Harlow died. I had tears in my eyes."

By the time she was fifteen, Cloris was in the Des Moines Little Theater in *Ah, Wilderness*, proving her talents so well that she received a scholarship to Northwestern University. She had beauty too, winning the Miss Chicago beauty crown and scoring as a runner-up in the Miss America contest. She became a member of Elia Kazan's Actors Studio. Jack L. Warner signed her but said she was "unphotographable" even though she was "a fine actress." They tried to improve her nose and her name, but she refused.

Despite Jack L. Warner, she persisted. Her first movie was *Kiss Me Deadly* (1955), a hard-boiled Mike Hammer private eye Film Noir drama that today is considered a mini-classic of its genre. She went

This is Cloris Leachman on the set of Creature Features *the day we taped an interview about* Herbie Goes Bananas.

This is me on my Creature Features *set, getting a handle on the head that Cloris Leachman described during our dungeon visit as "Poor little fella."*

on to work with Paul Newman in *The Rack* (1956), and with Efrem Zimbalist Jr. in *The Chapman Report* (1962). Then, there was her role as Agnes in *Butch Cassidy and the Sundance Kid* (1969) opposite Paul Newman. Bigger, better roles were hers in live TV on *Playhouse 90, Studio One,* and *Philco Playhouse*. This training ground brought her to the attention of the producers of *The Mary Tyler Moore Show*. For five seasons, she portrayed Phyllis Lindstrom, a busybody living in Mary's apartment building who eventually takes over the building when her husband Lars dies.

Lars' death triggered the release of the Lindstrom character in a spin off series that resulted in *Phyllis,* a CBS sitcom from 1975-1977. In the new format, Phyllis returns to her hometown of San Francisco, and, with a teenage daughter to support, she moves in with her mother and her second husband, a judge named Baxter. Strangely, the series was marked by a real-life death. Actress Barbara Colby, who played Julie Erskine, died one night in a senseless shooting in Westwood. The murder was never solved. Elderly actress Judith Lowry, playing Mother Dexter, was remarried during the second season but she and her new on-screen husband, Burt Mustin, both died of natural causes before the marriage episode was aired. This called for numerous format changes, and by the end of the second season, the network decided to drop the series.

Cloris is currently costarring in *The History of the World, Part I,* another crazed Mel Brooks comedy opus in which she portrays the Madame accredited with starting the French Revolution. "I operate this inn in a poor section of Paris. It is so poor that the beggars are begging among themselves. The sign on my shop reads, 'Serving the Scum of Paris for Over 300 Years.' And I greet all my customers the same: 'Bonjour, scum.' "

At that point in our conversation, Cloris' face twists into a scowling countenance, as if she is plotting a way to send some of her friends to the guillotine. She is no longer Cloris Leachman; she has become one of her own wild and crazy characters, shuffling up a flight of cobwebbed stairs, staying close to the candles, as one who knows that the staircase can be treacherous.

During her Bay Area visit, I also have the opportunity to have Cloris as a guest on my *Creature Features* show. I have proposed that during one of our segments, she and I will walk across my set and exchange some comedy lines. She agrees. We start out by walking to a guillotine, a major part of my set. She picks a severed head out of the basket, turns, and gives it to me. "Poor little fella," she says. I reply, "My producer. He's a basket case." She glares at me, then continues to walk toward a flight of steps leading to a dungeon cell. She turns with an object lying across her palm. "Let me give you a hand up the steps." The object is a severed human hand. Well, it's just a prop to add to the atmosphere of the guillotine set.

Viewers would later tell me it was one of the funniest moments in the series. But don't credit me. It was Cloris' doing.

Cloris Leachman in one of her zany movie roles, as Mrs. McFarland in the 1989 comedy-fantasy Prancer.

Since the day of our meeting, Cloris never stopped working in films and TV. She really scored big in 2006 when her performance opposite Ben Kingsley in the HBO movie, *Mrs. Harris*, brought her an Emmy nomination and a SAG Award nomination. That same year, she was given an honorary Doctorate in Fine Arts from Drake University. In 2011, she was inducted into the TV Academy Hall of Fame. This crazy, wonderful woman just never stops.

DICK SHAWN
Don't Shun Shawn–His Idea
Is To Have Fun in the Crazy House

Dick Shawn, a popular comedian, comes to San Francisco's Alcazar Theater to present a one-man play. Dick has been a successful nightclub comic, but now he's doing a drama about a comedian.

My wife and I arrive a half-hour before starting time and take our seats. There is no curtain across the stage, which is littered with piles of newspapers and other debris. As we sit waiting for the show to begin, I notice that one of the newspapers is rising and falling, as if something underneath is moving. I study the amount of debris and realize that it is high enough to conceal a human body beneath it. I come to the conclusion that it must be Dick Shawn under those papers, and I am correct.

When it's time for the curtain to go up, there is no curtain, but Shawn suddenly pops up and stands fully erect, and immediately draws a round of applause, especially from those who never realized he had been on the stage since they had arrived. It is one strange moment. I can't wait to get to an interview with Shawn. I just know I am in for something unusual. The play closes suddenly, and just as suddenly, Shawn returns for a new engagement at the Alcazar, and that's when my wish comes true.

Professionally and spiritually, the character of Jackie Clarke is a dying comedian. The world is changing drastically around him while he struggles to keep abreast by updating and re-evaluating his comedy material. Clarke no longer believes in himself. His timing is off, his punch lines are weak. He can't come to grips with his own reality.

So, he sleeps. He dreams he is Junior, a Las Vegas dynamo capable of everything from rock 'n roll to juggling oranges to reciting long passages of Shakespeare.

Jackie awakens. He is uninspired; he only slides deeper into ineptitude and failure. Finally, he turns into a tragic, pathetic figure, a victim of our complicated times.

Dick Shawn

Doesn't exactly sound like the makings of a comedy show, does it? Yet Dick Shawn, as Jackie Clarke, manages to turn *The Second Greatest Entertainer in the Whole Wide World* into a rich, multi-layered one-man show that is allegorical and brimming with historical and sociological satire. Always devastating, always funny. Shawn blends these seemingly non-homogenous ingredients with a deft wit and a sense of timing that occasionally borders on genius.

The Second Greatest Entertainer in the Whole Wide World first played at the Alcazar Theater in San Francisco to audience capacity. Shawn then closed the show briefly to fulfill a Las Vegas engagement, but this week [December 1977] has returned to the Alcazar for another month-long run.

I tell Shawn about seeing his earlier show and discovering that he was on the stage before the show begins, covered by newspapers.

"I do that," he responds, "because no other actor or comedian has ever done anything like it. I love to surprise my audience, to lure them away from the commonplace into an arena where perhaps the human soul has never gone before.

"Each person who comes to the theater," Shawn tells me, "brings with him a different state of mind. The first thing I try to do, through a form of distraction and agitation, is to break down those mental barriers and defenses and strip everyone of their so-called sophistication. Then I'm working with a unit."

That's when Clarke/Shawn begins to eat the banana. "If you want to interpret that as an evolutionary bit, fine. I try to touch into areas most nightclub comedians don't explore because the underlying theme is not funny. A-bombs, religion, the foul air we breath, Armageddon, the Nixon Administration."

Shawn explains that his cabaret/theater concept sprang out of frustration. "I've been a nightclub comedian most of my career, but I learned early in the game that club audiences don't necessarily come to be entertained. They don't want to have to think. I found out just how unpopular a comedian can be when I used to crack a lot of anti-Nixon jokes before Watergate. One of the clubs in Vegas didn't invite me back, presumably because I had offended some of the high rollers. But theater audiences ... now there's a different crowd. They come to be entertained, and they don't mind working for some of it. When I talk with people, I realize they're reading extra things into the material; they see things I hadn't purposely intended."

Shawn insists that "all humor is based on some form of hostility, but it needs to be sweetened a little, so it's palatable for an audience. And irony . . . you must be able to look at the fact that all the lawbreakers who served under Nixon are now making millions from their books and their lecture series, while the night watchmen who blew the first whistle on them can't even find a job."

Many have commented on Shawn's "off the wall" form of comedy, which often seems ad libbed and spontaneous. "I do a certain amount of ad libbing if the audience response is just so, but basically what I'm doing is a set piece of theater that can't be tampered with very much."

Shawn remains on the stage during the intermission, stretched out flat on his back, seemingly asleep. I ask him to explain.

"I'm about 80 per cent out of it," he says. "I'm not on any kind of head trip, I'm just relaxing. People usually don't bother me; they don't have time and still go to the toilet. One night, a lady brought me a cookie and pressed it into my hand and blessed me. But otherwise, there's been no incidents."

Shawn admits that *The Second Greatest Entertainer in the Whole Wide World* is autobiographic in part and briefly describes its history. "I tried the show first at Florida State University, where the students received the idea warmly. I was happy at such a positive response, but on the other hand, the college view is not necessarily a clue to commercial acceptance, so I took the show to Boston and mounted a production for $5,000. I was scheduled for three weeks but stayed ten. One critic called it 'one of the ten best plays of the year.' I decided I had to be doing something right so I went to the Promenade Theater off-Broadway for several months. Now that San Francisco has received me well, I plan to take the show to Los Angeles after I close here."

Shawn sums it up thusly: "The idea is for me and the audience to have fun together in the crazy house called the theater."

Dick Shawn had only ten more years to live. During that time, he continued to guest on TV series. His most lasting would be in 1985 in *Hail to the Chief* as a Russian character named Ivan Zolotov. He often appeared at celebrity roasts. At a Playboy event honoring Tommy Chong, Shawn went through the motions of vomiting a soup all over himself, another example of his unusual style of behavior. It is utterly ironic that in 1987, while Shawn was performing his show at Mandeville Hall at the University of California at San Diego, he suddenly fell to the stage in the middle of a monologue. The audience, thinking it part of the act, laughed and applauded. Even those backstage thought it was part of Shawn's usual behavior. Unfortunately, as he lay there in the middle of the stage, he died of a heart attack. He was sixty-three.

BOB NEWHART
The Monologue Comedian
Who Grew Into TV Sitcoms
–All Named After Him

Narrow lanes of bubbles work their way to the top of the glass. Bob Newhart sips at the Pepsi-Cola gently, letting only a small amount pass through his lips. Setting the glass aside, he gazes through the window of his seventh-floor Fairmont Hotel suite down onto the city of San Francisco.

In June 1967, a crisp sunny extra warm Saturday morning, Newhart is obviously enjoying not only the view that takes in Coit Tower, the two bridges, and Alcatraz Island, but the sounds drifting up through a partially opened side window.

Newhart has spent most of the night before traveling on a train from Los Angeles, and now he can lean back in his chair, his tie removed, his white shirt unbuttoned at the throat, his youthful face as placid as his manner.

Bob Newhart

In a few hours he will once again be on a train, heading over the Sierra to Reno, Nevada, where he will begin an engagement at Harold's Club. It means the anxiety and feverish pace that accompanies each opening night, but right now the thirty-seven-year-old comedian seems to be trying to soak up as much of the room's serenity as he can.

"You want to know what my main shtick is?" A pause while he brushes a speck from a cuff-link. "I think it's attitude. By that I mean . . . well, I take a character and establish his point-of-view. All my skits are basically situations and man's reaction to them. I never permit a character to lose the validity of what he believes, and I make him work against the surroundings. Abrasion.

"For example, my janitor calls his boss to tell him that a giant gorilla is on the rooftop, attacking airplanes. The attitude is that the job of sweeping and cleaning must be fulfilled, no matter how ludicrous the circumstances. And the attitude smacks of fear—fear that he won't be able to complete his work and keep the boss pleased as that monster threatens mankind.

"Fear or self-preservation is a chief ingredient in many of my sketches. I once counted thirty-five examples I could give you. I don't conceive a situation with fear in mind, but I always go back to make sure it's there. Fear is a plentiful source of material. Yes, I suppose I have fears myself. I don't go to a psychiatrist yet, but I'd say I have enough to be considered healthy."

A knob turns. Out of an adjoining room comes Newhart's red-headed wife, Virginia, daughter of actor William Quinn and mother of Newhart's two children. She is searching for her make-up. Has anyone seen it? Unable to find the cosmetics, she takes a seat and crosses her legs.

By then, Newhart is discussing comedy sketches that fail. "Believe me, only one out of every three works. And of the five or six in my head at this moment, I'd say only one, two at the most, will pan out. I did a department store bit once that lasted seven minutes, and I didn't get a single snicker or guffaw.

"Audiences are as unpredictable as new material. Each group, I try to size up in the first five minutes, so I can select material that would seem to best suit it. You know, colleges provide excellent audiences, and I only wish I had more time to devote to that circuit. Students seem to be more in tune with what's happening. I guess it's because they're still idealists—haven't been beaten down yet like the rest of us adults."

Who has helped the most in influencing his style of comedy?

Hardly a pause, then, "Robert Benchley, Max Schulman, Laurel and Hardy. Those four I rank the highest. As to how they've influence me, I would be hard put to say. I can only assure you they have, for I was too admiring of them in my younger years.

Others?

"The Marx Brothers, W. C. Fields, Fred Allen. These are men who never lost their appeal, who are as funny today as in their own time. As for contemporaries, I enjoy Bob and Ray, Jonathan Winters, Buddy Hackett, the Smothers Brothers, even from Milton Berle, I've learned a thing or two."

Is he partial to any up-and-coming comedians?

"Of course Bill Cosby has already arrived. Flip Wilson is another I'm watching with keen interest. You know, I admire them all. I know that sounds Pollyannaish, but I have respect for my counterparts because I believe we're all in the hardest area of show business. There's nothing tougher than dying as a comedian."

"Yes," chimes in Virginia, who has been listening keenly, as if she is hearing Newhart's thoughts for the first time. "Comedians are the most loyal of all performers. One will do anything he can to help another, even though they still compete with each other like crazy."

There is no hesitation to my next question: What have been the most memorable moments in your career since it started in 1960?

"Three moments. First, the Emmy Award Show in '61, when I won for my TV comedy series. Second, performing at President Kennedy's birthday party; and third, a command performance before Queen Elizabeth."

He continues, "I think the important thing to take away is that comedians need the perspective of children. Inhibitions deaden most adults, preventing us from doing those things we would like to try.

"Take a young woman in a low-cut dress. When she enters a room, we men would like to ogle her, but instead we turn away, sneaking an occasional glance when she isn't looking. A child would look outright. Well, a comedian should 'look outright.' And when a comedian can achieve this fresh perspective, he has achieved an element of successful comedy."

What are the provisions of his current contract with NBC?

Newhart flashes a toothy smile. "I never thought you'd ask. Well, it means I'll be replacing Johnny Carson for six weeks this summer on *The Tonight Show*. Then, of course, I'll be doing guest shots with Perry Como, Dean Martin, and many others. The best part is, I'll be starring in my own variety-comedy series soon. I refuse to lower my standards for quality material, so I'm still working on a suitable format, one which will not drain me after a few weeks. You can be sure I won't compromise."

Virginia smiles. "Of that," she says, "you can be doubly sure."

Bob Newhart's career doesn't really begin to flourish until the fall of 1972, when *The Bob Newhart Show* premieres on CBS. Because he is scheduled to perform in the Bay Area, and I happen to be making a trip to Last Vegas, Nevada, arrangements are made for me to meet the comedian in the gambling mecca in March 1973.

Bob has had a difficult afternoon at the Las Vegas Country Club. Not that there's anything wrong with his golf swing or his par . . . if it were only that simple. No, his problem this day is all about his "swinging partner," Don Rickles, the comedian who loves to humiliate members of his audience with a never-ending series of put-downs. And today it's Bob who would like to "put down" Rickles.

After each hole, with Bob consistently leading by at least three strokes, a pause is in order while Bob bolsters Don's flagging spirits. If Bob cannot instill new confidence in Rickles, he might refuse to continue. Such an ordeal can indeed play havoc with your game, not to mention your afternoon.

Now the game is done, the golf bags are back in their respective closets, and Bob has returned to the Sands Hotel, where he is appearing in the Copa Room with Florence Henderson.

He won't have to put up with Rickles again until the dinner they've planned to devour between shows. So Bob, for the first time in a while, looks relieved as he lounges in the Presidential Suite located behind the main hotel.

Two of Bob's children, Robert and Timothy, are ravenously cleaning the trays of food that have just been delivered to them by room service. Two-year-old Jennifer hurries past, carrying a miniature green toy. Bob, who is just getting dressed for his first show of the evening, leads the way into the bedroom. He motions his head toward a blaring TV set (Las Vegas used-car salesmen, he remarks, are about as loud as they come), closes the door, and takes a seat at a bare table. Virginia (or Ginnie), his wife whom I had met during our previous interview together, will look after the kids while we talk.

Bedlam having been cut short, Bob becomes totally relaxed, conveying the same gentleness and ease he projects on stage. Although now a sitcom TV star, he has lost none of his modesty or charm. Bob, one assumes and hopes, will always remain Bob Newhart.

"I've had the stardom," he begins. "I've had the Emmies and the recognition, and I know the feeling isn't all that great. The main problem is, there's never enough time to enjoy stardom. Or whatever you choose to call it. You end up working every waking moment, and pretty soon you begin to realize there are some things far more important. Like time spent with the family, or time off to go somewhere where you can be alone with your wife for a few hours. Make that days."

The fact that his family is with him on this Vegas gig is not unusual. Whenever possible, Ginnie and the children tag right along. Bob shakes his head and states emphatically, "In the end, I would never let my career interfere with my private life. Nothing is worth having to have to work seven days a week."

Doing this Vegas gig, in fact, is almost like a vacation for Bob. Unlike the restrictions and long hours of the TV series, he finds that doing only two shows a night is a snap. Golf in the daytime, plenty of rest at night or early in the morning. "You can't beat it."

Since his first comedy album was released in 1960, Bob has remained a monologue comedian. While he has never indulged in the stinging satire of Lenny Bruce or Mort Sahl, nor in the free-for-all antics of Jonathan Winters or Red Skelton, he has polished his own easy-going style in which he takes a situation and gently builds a routine around it.

San Francisco critic Ralph J. Gleason once described Newhart as "only pleasantly amusing, never belly-laugh funny," a comedian who "never ventures into the areas of taboo."

Well, that may have been true six or seven years ago, but Bob has been liberalized with the times. His material is now far more suggestive (one new routine is concerned with a police line-up of all-nude males) and he is not reluctant to become slightly sacrilege when he touches on today's changing religious mores. Still, he relies on updated monologues and devotes one part of each show to doing some of his old favorites from his "Button Down" days. Audiences are responding to them and Bob's underplayed delivery with frequent belly laughs.

He admits he is tough on material. "I'm probably one of the hardest people to write for. In the final analysis, about 90 per cent of my stuff is conceived on the stage. People tend to laugh at what's true, they like to laugh at themselves. The violators of what I'm describing are the ones who laugh the hardest. But I've got to start with a sound premise. Something steeped in fact, or based on the realities of human nature. Otherwise, I'm dead."

One of the first things Bob does when he steps onto a stage is feel out the audience with certain key lines. "There's a period of time between the pay-off line delivery and the laughs. It may be only one-half of a second, but after you've done a few hundred shows it seems like four minutes. And this will oftentimes influence my choice of material for the rest of the show. Some audiences are geared to fast monologues or routines; some are geared for slower material. I have to talk, listen, revise, and then start to do my real show."

Bob confesses uncertainty about what motivates him, and where his career is leading him. "I have this theory that when you retire, you discover why you devoted your life to show business. Everything before retirement is rationalization and guess work. You say you're in it for the money or the fame or something, but who really knows? As for the future, I'd say most of it will be devoted to nightclub and concert dates. I've done some film work. Let's see, there was Cold *Turkey* [1971], *Hot Millions* (1968), *Hell Is for Heroes* (1962), and I just finished a TV-film, *Thursday's Game*, with Gene Wilder. But I miss the audience. I worked for three months on *Catch-22* (1970), but there was never that response, that reaction a comedian immediately needs.

"Records? I haven't cut a new disc in about five years. The market just isn't there anymore. Also, you're giving your material away on a record. It's self-defeating because people become too familiar with your material and tend not to show up for the live shows."

And his TV series?

"Coming in behind Mary Tyler Moore on CBS in the Saturday night time slot doesn't hurt us a bit. Casting and writing are essential; they go hand in hand; you just can't separate them. The mail has indicated viewers appreciate the fact there are no precocious children, dogs, cats, or a link-headed husband. Suzanne Pleshette and I have tried to make an adult relationship out of it. Tried to make it something more than another sit comedy. You may recall the bedroom antics in our pilot show."

Bob stands up and stretches, shrugging his shoulders. "But TV is hard work. I don't have that freedom of movement. I feel confined to those three cameras." He leads the way toward the front door. The sound of his children can be heard as they romp near the TV set, which is still blaring.

Showtime is approaching for Bob. Ginnie has to finish getting dressed. Then, there's that between-shows dinner with Don Rickles to look forward to. "Like I said, I'd never let it get the best of me, this sitcom thing. Nothing is more important than all this surrounding me right now. Wife, kids."

Jennifer, the two-year-old, wanders past her father, still clutching her small green toy. Bob pats her gently on the head, smiles at her, and says goodbye. She smiles right back, and tells daddy to hurry back. She'll miss him.

Sitcoms never seem to stop for Bob, and always named after him, no matter how fictional. *The Bob Newhart Show* continued through 1978, for which he was nominated twice for a Golden Globe Award. Then in 1982, in a series simply entitled *Newhart*, he became Dick Loudon, a Vermont innkeeper who will deal with marital and business issues through 1988, and also become a Vermont TV personality. For this he is nominated for four Golden

Globes and one Emmy. In 1992-1993, he starred in *Bob,* portraying a cartoonist who has created a superhero. The show was short-lived compared to his previous series. Also short-lived was *Bob and George* (1997-98). Since then, plenty of TV roles. It still isn't stopping.

Index

—A—

Abbott and Costello (team), 183
Ace Crawford, Private Eye (TV), 149-154
Actors Studio, The, 205
Adams, Don aka Donald James Yarmy), 1, 42, 108-109, 111, 116-122
Adler, Barry, v
Adler, Evelyn, v
Adventures of Sherlock Holmes' Smarter Brother (film), 184
Agent 86 aka Maxwell Smart (character), 108-109, 111, 114-115, 118-122
Agent 99 (character), 108-109, 111, 114
Ah, Wilderness (play), 205
Aiello, Danny, 73
Albright, Lola, 152
Alcatraz Island, 214
Alcazar Theater, The, 209, 211
Alda, Alan, 75
Alice in Wonderland (film), 186
Allen, Fred, 216
Allen, Gracie, 9, 15, 128
Allen, Irwin, 192
Allen, Steve, 19, 121, 147, 153
All Hands on Deck (film), 191
All in the Family (TV), 87, 100-107
Alpert, Herb, 101
Alschuler, Susan, 70
Altamira Hotel, 163
Altman, Robert, 75
Anderson, Ernie ala Ghoulardi, x, 153, 155-159
Andrews, Julie, 75
Andy Griffith Show, The (TV), 19, 21, 30, 42
Anne of Cleves, 10
Ansara, Matthew, 192
Ansara, Michael, 191-193
Archer, Beverly, 140
Archie Bunker's Place (TV), 103, 107

Arden, Eve, 160
Arkin, Alan, 69-71, 73
Armstrong Circle Theater (TV), 107
Armstrong, Louis, viii
Arnaz, Desi, ix
Arthur, Beatrice, 87, 92, 96
Association, The (rock 'n roll), 123
Auntie Mame (play), 80
Autry, Gene, 136, 174
Avengers, The (TV), 108
Avery, Tex, 54
Aykroyd, Dan, 63

—B—

Bacall, Lauren, 222
Bachelor Party (film), 63
Bagdad Café (TV), 107
Bain, Conrad, 93-97
Bain, Monica, 94, 97
Balcutha, The (ship), 31
Ball, Lucille, ix, 161. 164-165
Band of Brothers (TV), 66
Banducci, Enrico, 30-32
Banff School of Fine Arts, 96
Barbary Coast (TV), 47
Barbeau, Adrienne, x, 85-94
Bardelli's Restaurant, 38, 130, 132, 179, 183
Bardot, Brigitte, 9
Barty, Billy, 150
Bay Area Classic Learning (Elderhostel), 197
Beach, Scott, 73
Bell, Book and Candle (film), 80
Bells Are Ringing (play), 107
Benchley, Robert, 216
Benny, Jack, 10, 60, 160, 200
Bergen, Candice, 182
Berle, Milton, x, 216
Berman, Joshua, 4
Berman, Shelley, 2-7, 28, 30, 197

Berry, Ken, 143
Bertha the Elephant, 182
Best Little Whorehouse in Texas, The (film), 26
Best of Jim Murray, The (book), 119
Big (film), 63-64
Bill Dana Show, The (TV), 121
Bimbo's 365 Club, 28, 36, 195, 198
Blackburn, Gary, v
Blackburn, Jean, v
Blaines, David, 157
Blanc, Mel, 1
Blau, Roger, 120
Blazing Saddles (film), 183
Bloch, Robert, 222
Bloom, John Irving aka Joe Bob Briggs, x, 155
Bob (TV), 221
Bob and George (TV), 221
Bob & Ray, 216
Bob Newhart Show, The (TV), 217, 220
Bogart, Humphrey, 145, 150
Bonanza (TV),
Bond, James (character), 44, 46, 48, 108
Bosom Buddies (TV), 58, 60-63
Boston Legal (TV), 7
Boyett, Bob, 58
Bradbury, Ray, 222
Brady Bunch, The (TV), 138
Brady, Pat, 176
Brand New Life, A (TV), 203
Brass Bottle, The (film), 191-192
Brinegar, Paul, 222
Briggs, Joe Bob aka John Irving Bloom, x, 155-157
Broccoli, Albert, 48
Brooklyn Tabernacle Choir, 17
Brooks, Mel, 108, 114, 121, 179-183, 202, 204, 207
Brooks, James, 138
Brothers, The (TV), 160
Bruce, Lenny, 2, 7, 28, 196-197, 218

Buckley, Lord, 196
Buck Rogers (comic strip), 55
Bugs Bunny (character), 1, 49-50, 52-57, 136
Bugs Bunny on Broadway (concert), 56
Burnett, Carol, 19, 68-76, 140-143, 145-148
Burnett, Carrie, 70, 76
Burnett, Smiley,
Burns, Allan, 138
Burns, George, ix, 8-10, 15, 145
Burns and Schreiber, 195
Burns, Jack, 195
Butch Cassidy and the Sundance Kid (film), 206

—C—
Cadwallader, Stan, 26-27
Caesar, Sid, viii-ix, 6, 183
Caesar's Palace (Las Vegas), 36
Call Me Mister (film), 200
Cambridge, Godfrey, 7, 30
Camellia Room (Fairmont Hotel), 120, 188, 191
Campbell, Glen, 133
Campton Place Hotel, 77
Cannon, Jimmy, 119
Cannonball II (film), 26
Capitol Records, 39
Captain Nice (TV), 108
Captain Phillips (film), 67
Carlin, George, 194-197
Carnegie Tech (drama school), 112
Carney, Art, ix
Carnival Cruise Lines, 42
Carnivale (TV), 93
Carol & Company (TV), 76
Carol Burnett Show, The (TV), 71-72, 140, 142, 145-147, 154, 158
Carpenter, John, x, 88, 91
Carpenter, John Cody, 88, 91-92
Carson, Johnny, 40, 196, 217
Carter, Howard, 157
Casey at the Bat (cartoon), 186

Castle, William, 222
Catch-22 (film), 220
Cavett, Dick, 30
CBS Studio Center, 136
CBS Television City, 104-105, 123, 126, 130
Cedar Jack (cowboy), 177
Champion, Gower, 12
Chandler, Jeff, 152
Chandler, Raymond, 150
Channing, Carol, 8-16, 191
Chaplin, Charlie, 52, 126
Chapman Report, The (film), 206
Charley's Aunt (play), 60
Charley's Aunt (film), 60
Chateau Marmont, 108
Cheap Detective, The (film), 80
Check Is in the Mail, The (film), 39
Cher (TV), 203
Chief, The aka Agent Q (character), 108, 114-116
Chong, Tommy, 212
Chouinard Art Institute, 53
Christie, Dick, 152
Chu Chu and the Philly Flash (film), 68-71, 75
Chuckamuck: The Life and Times of an Animated Cartoonist (book), 49-52
Cincinnati Conservatory of Music, 116
Circle Gallery, 49
Circle Star Theater, 24
City Lights (film), 126
Clampett, Bob, 54
Clark, Jackie, (character), 209-211
Clark, Ron, 152
Clift Hotel (San Francisco), 11
Clouseau, Inspector (character), 108
Coca, Imogene, ix
Coco, James, x, 77-84
Cohen, Myron, 7
Coit Tower, 214
Cold Turkey (film), 107
Colby, Barbara, 207
Cold Turkey (film), 219
Colonna, Jerry, x, 185-187
Comedy Central, 197
Committee, The (comedy team), 196
Como, Perry, 217
Conklin, Osgood (character), 160
Conway, Tim aka Thomas Daniel Conway, 71, 101, 148-155, 157-158
Conway, Tom, 153
"Cool Water" (song), 174, 177
Copa Room, The, 217
Copperfield, David, 157
Corey, Professor Irwin, 30
Cosby, Bill, 30, 216
"Crate, The" (film episode), 92
Craven, Wes, 91
Crazy Guggenheim (character), 198-199
Creature Features (TV), viii, x, 40-41, 202, 205-206
Creature Features Movie Guide Strikes Again, The (book), 222
Creepshow (film), 92
Crosby, Bing, ix, 185-186
Curb Your Enthusiasm (TV), 7
Curd, Dick, 116
Curtis, Ken, 1, 174-178
Curtis, Tony, 60
Custer, General George Armstrong, 98

—D—

Daffy Duck (cartoon), 50, 53-55
Dallas Times Herald, The, 155
Damn Yankees (play), 107
Dana, Barbara, 70
Danese, Shera, 150
Dark Shadows (TV), 96
Daugherty, George, 55
Day, Doris, 166, 196
Damn Yankees (play), 107
Davidson, John, 133
Day, Dennis, 160
Day to Day Affair (TV), 80
Dean Martin Show, The (TV), 181

Dektar, Clilff, v
Del Mar High School, 90
DeLuise, Dom, 145, 148, 179-184
Desilu Studios, ix
Des Moines Little Theater, 205
"Diamonds Are a Girl's Best Friend" (song), 14
Dick, Andy, 122
The Dick Van Dyke Show (TV), 136, 138-139, 147
Dietrich, Marlene, 9
Diff'rent Strokes (TV), 97
Diller, Phyllis aka Mrs. Sherman "Fang" Diller, 31, 166-173
Dinosaurs (TV), 103
Disney, Walt, viii, x, 54, 150, 150, 186, 204
Dixon, Donna, 60
Dom DeLuise Show, The (TV), 181
Dominique the Great (character), 179
Don Adams' Screen Test (TV), 122
Don't Drink the Water (play), 5
Dorchester Hotel, 10
Down to Earth (TV), 38
Dracula (character), 46
Dragnet (1987 film), 63
Dr. Seuss' How the Grinch Stole Christmas (film), 55
Duck Amuck (cartoon), 54
Duck Dodgers in the 24 · Century (cartoon), 55
Dunes Hotel (Las Vegas), 10
Dunn, Michael, 47
DuPont Show of the Week, 4
Dutch Treat (film), 39

—E—

East Side, West Side (TV), 112
Eastwood, Clint, 222
Eden, Barbara aka Barbara Huffman, 188-193
Edie Hart (character), 152
Edwards, Blake, 150
Eegah (film), 44

Elderhostel (Road Scholar), viii
Elizabeth Holloway School of Theater, 191
Elvira aka Cassandra Peterson (horror hostess), x, 156-157, 159, 222
Enrico's (restaurant), 31, 38
Ephron, Nora, 66
Escape From New York (film), 91
"Everybody Loves Somebody Sometime" (song),

—F—

Fail-Safe (film), 182
Fairmont Hotel, 68, 120, 188, 214
Falana, Lola, 133
Farrow, Mia, 204
Father Fyodor (character), 179
Feldon, Barbara, 1, 108-113, 115, 118
Festus (character), 1, 176
Fibber McGee and Molly Show, The (radio), x, 160, 163-164
Fiddler on the Roof (play), 86
Fields, Totie, 35
Fields, W. C., 33, 196, 216
First Traveling Saleslady, The (film), 10
Fisher, Shug, 176
Fitz and Bones (TV), 132
Five Weeks in a Balloon (film), 192
Flash and the Firecat (film), 48
Fleagle Gang, The (outlaws), 177
Flintstone Kids (TV), 38
Flipper (TV), 112
Florida State University, 212
Fog, The (film), 91
Foggy Williams (character), 160
Follies, The (play), 15
Fontaine, Frank, 198-201
Fontaine, Ray, 198
Ford, Glenn, 117, 181
Ford, John, 174-175
For Scentimental Reasons (cartoon), 59
Foul Play (TV), 62
Four Seasons, The (film), 75
Franklyn, Milton, 55

Frau Blucher (character), 202
Frawley, Bill, 164
Fred Frump (character), 201
Freleng, Isadore (Friz), 54
Fresno (TV), 76
Friendly Fire (film), 72
From Hare to Eternity (cartoon), 57
Frontier, The (Las Vegas), 36
Front Page, The (film), 75

—G—

Gang That Shot Up Hollywood, The (book), 222
Garford C. Hogue (character), 39
"Gargoyle" (TV episode), 91
Garner, James, 75
Garner, Smokey (janitor), 52
Garson, Greer, 124-125
Gay Purr-ee (film), 55
Gentlemen Prefer Blondes (play), 9-10, 14
George Burns' One-Man Show (TV),
Getaway, The (film), 101
Get Smart (TV), 1, 108-122
Get Smart (second series), 122
Ghoulardi (horror host), x, 156-159
Gilford, Jack, 80
Gilmore Girls (TV), 103
Gingold, Hermione, 74
Glass-Bottom Boat, The (film), 182
Gleason, Jackie, ix, 5, 63, 183, 195-196, 199-201
Gleason, Ralph J., 219
Gloria (TV), 103
Godmothers, The (film), 201
Golden Gate Bridge, The, 163
Goman, Ray K., v
Gomer Pyle–USMC (TV), 1, 19-24, 26, 28-31, 38, 42-43
Gone With the Wind (film), 149
Good Morning, World (TV), 32
Gordon, Gale, x, 160-165
Gordon, Ruth, 74
Gordon, Virginia, 163

Governor and J. J., The (TV), 117
Grant, Cary, 32
Grass Is Greener Over the Septic Tank, The (TV), 73
Grease (play), 86-88
Great Adventure, The (TV), 21
Great Lakes Shakespeare Festival, 61
Greco, Buddy, 195
Greene, Shecky, 7, 33, 133
Gregory, Dick, 2, 7
Griffin, Merv, 195
Griffith, Andy, 1, 23-24, 32
Gunsmoke (TV), 1, 176-178

—H—

Hackett, Buddy, 7, 79
Hagman, Larry, 192
Hail to the Chief (TV), 212
Hall, Arch Jr., 44
Hall, Barbara Anne aka Barbara Feldon, 112
Hamburger Hamlet, 141
Hamilton, Joseph, 73, 142
Hammer, Mike (character), 205
Hammett, Dashiell, 150
Hanks, Tom, 56-67
Hardy, Oliver, 183
Hargrove, Marion, 20
Harlow, Jean, 205
Harold's Club (Reno), 214
Harrah's Tahoe, 8, 185
Harrah's Club (Reno), 119
Harrah's Lounge (Lake Tahoe), 186
Harryhausen, Ray, 222
Haunted Honeymoon (film), 183-184
Have Gun–Will Travel (TV), 175
Hayworth, Rita, 72
Head, Edith, 166
Health (film), 75
He Knows You're Alone (film), 62
Hell Is for Heroes (film), 219
Hello, Dolly! (play), 5, 10-13, 15
"Hello, My Baby" (song), 55

Henderson, Bill, 150
Henderson, Florence, 217
Henry, Buck, 108, 114, 121
Henry Hawk (character), 50
Henry VIII, 10
Herbie (movie series), x
Herbie Goes Bananas (film), 202, 205
Herbie Goes to Monte Carlo (film), 202
Herbie Rides Again (film), 202
Here Comes the Groom (film), 200
Here's Lucy (TV), 161, 165
Herman, Jerry, 15
High Anxiety (film), 202, 204
High Rise aka *Someone Is Watching* (TV), 91
High Sierra Tahoe, 38, 40
History of the World, Part I (film), 207
Hitchcock, Alfred, 73
Holly Golightly (play), 139
Hollywood Brown Derby, The, 85
Hollywood Squares, The (TV),
Honeymooners, The (TV), x
Hoover Hot Shots, The, 174
Hope, Bob, ix-x, 133, 170-171, 183, 185-187
Horn, The (club), 19, 21
Horton Hears a Who (cartoon), 55
Hotel Meredien, 91
Hot Millions (film), 219
Houdini, 157
House of the Damned, The (film), 47-48
Howard, Moe, 1
How to Marry a Millionaire (TV), 191
Hudson, Rock, 27
Human Duplicators, The (film), 47
hungry i, (club), 30-31, 33, 35, 38, 40
Hunk (film), 81
Hustler, The (film),
Hyatt on Union Square, 44-46

—I—

Ice House, The (comedy club), 127-128
Iceman Cometh, The (play), 61, 96

I Dream of Jeannie (TV), 188-190, 192-193
I Hate Everybody . . . Starting With Me (book),
I Love Lucy (TV), 164-165
I Love My Wife (play), 132
Inspector Gadget (TV), 122
I Spy (TV), 30
Ives, Burl, 192
I Was a TV Horror Host (book), 222
Iworks, Ub, 54

—J—

Jack Benny Program, The (TV), 200
Jackie Gleason Show, The (TV), 198-199
James Bond 007: Everything or Nothing (video game), 48
James Coco Diet, The (book), 77-78
Jaws (character), 44, 46-48
Jeffersons, The (TV), 84
Jessel, Georgie, 7
Jim Nabors Hour, The (TV), 24-25, 33, 38
Jim Nabors Show, The (TV), 26
Joe the Bartender (character), 198-199
Joe Versus the Volcano (film), 63-64
John Scott Trotter's Orchestra, 185
Jones, Chuck, 1, 49-57
Jordan, Jim, 160, 164
Jordan, Marian, 160, 164
Jourdan, Louis, 132
Juilliard School of Music, 116
Just Lucky, I Guess: A Memoir of Sorts (book), 16

—K—

Kastner, Peter, 60
Katmandu (TV), 143
Kaye, Danny, 5, 147
Kazan, Elia, 205
Keaton, Buster, 52
Keith, Brian, 196
Kennedy, President John F., 216
Kiel, Richard, 44-48
King's Four-in-One Restaurant, 145
Kingsley, Ben, 208

King's Mare (play), 10
Kingston Trio, The, 30
Kiss Me Deadly (film), 205
Kleinberg, David, v, viii, 83-84, 197
Klinger (*M*A*S*H* character), 60
Klute (film), 107
Korman, Harvey, 141, 144-148, 154, 204
Kraft Music Hall, The (radio), 185
KTVU (Channel 2, Oakland), 40-41
KTVU's 30th Anniversary Special (TV), 40-41

—L—

Ladies' Home Journal (magazine), 70
Lady Macbeth, 9, 191
Laine, Frankie, 222
Langella, Frank, 179
Lanza, Mario, 198
Last Days of Mussolini, The (painting), 127
Last of the Red Hot Lovers (play), 80
Last of the Secret Agents, The (film), 147
Last Picture Show, The (film), 203
Las Vegas Country Club, 217
Laurel and Hardy, 33, 157, 183, 216
Laverne and Shirley (TV), 143
Lawrence, Vicki, 140-144
Leachman, Cloris, x, 202-208
Leachman Lumber Corporation, The, 204
League of Their Own, A (film), 63-64
Lear, Norman, 87, 93, 96, 104
Lee, Christopher, 222
Lee. Lorelei (character), 9-10, 14
Lemmon, Jack, 60
Levi, Dolly (character), 10, 13-14, 16
Lewes, Samantha, 61-62
Lieutenant, The (TV), 19
Life With Lucy (TV), 165
Lincoln High School (San Francisco), 191
Lindstrom, Phyllis (character), 206
Linke, Bettina, 42
Linke, Richard O., 34-36, 42
Liston, Sonny, 119

Little Red Riding Hood (character), 200
Little, Rich, 145, 148
Loco James (character), 191
Longest Yard, The (film), 48
Longshot, The (film), 148
Looney Tunes (cartoons), 54
Loos, Anita, 10, 14
Lord Buckley, 196
Lord Love a Duck (film), 147
Los Angeles Music Center, 106
Lost in Time and Space With Lefty Feep (book), 222
Loudon, Dick (character), 220
Love Boat, The (TV), 130, 158
Love Bug, The (film), 202
Love Bug Series (film), 202
Lowe, Charles, 12, 15-16
Lowry, Judith, 207
Lucy Show, The (TV), 161
Lugosi, Bela, 46
Lullaby (play), 106

—M—

Madame Curie (film), 125
Magic Castle, The, x, 156
Magnum Force (film), 222
Making It Big in the Movies (book), 48
Malden, Karl, 222
Malinger, Ross, 66
Mama's Family (TV), 141-142
Mandeville Hall (UC of San Diego), 213
Mandrake, The (play), 62
Man From U.N.C.L.E., The (TV), 108
Man in One Red Shoe, The (film), 65
Manning, Marilyn, 44
Man of La Mancha (film), 80
March Hare (character), 186
Marvin Marsh (character), 50
Marsh, Marvin (character), 50
Marie, Rose, 153
"Marionettes Inc." (TV episode), 80
Marshall, Gary, 143

Martin, Dean, 75, 217
Martin, Steve, 7, 19
Martin, Tony, 199
Marx Brothers, The, 216
Marx, Chico, 53
Marx, Groucho, 53
Maslin, Janet, 155
Mary Tyler Moore Show, The (TV), 136-139, 203, 206
*M*A*S*H* (TV), 60
Maslin, Janet, 155
Matchmaker, The (play), 16
Matlock (TV), 42
Matthau, Walter, 75
Maude (TV), x, 86-88, 90, 92, 94-97
May, Elaine, 2
Mayor LaTrivia (character), x, 160, 162-163
McCarthy, Joseph, 6
McClanahan, Rue, 143
McHale's Navy (TV), 154
McKimson, Robert, 54
Meadows, Audrey, x
Meet the Fokkers (film), 7
Merrill, Bob, 70
Michael Shayne, Private Detective (radio), 152
Michigan J. Frog (character), 55
Milkis, Ed, 58
Miller, Tom, 58
Miranda, Carmen, 69
Mitchum, Robert, 222
Monroe, Marilyn, 9
Moody, Ron, 179
Moonraker (film), 48
Moore, Dudley, 75
Moore, Mary Tyler, 136-139, 220
Moose Moran (character), 47
Mozart, Wolfgang Amadeus, 57
Mr. President (TV), 97
Mr. Smith Goes to Washington (TV), 21
Mrs. Doubtfire (film), 57
Mrs. Harris (TV), 208
Mrs. Miniver (film), 125
Mull, Martin, 132
Muppets Take Manhattan, The (film), 80
Murder By Death (film), 80
Murphy, Audie, 34
Murray, Jim, 119-120
Mustin, Burt, 207

—N—

Nabors, Jim, 1, 17-28, 30-31, 33-37, 42, 132
Napoleon, 98
Nasty Rabbit, The (film), 47
Nederlander, James, 15
New Fack's (night club), 31
Newhart (TV), 220
Newhart, Bob, 7, 214-221
Newhart, Jennifer, 218, 220
Newhart, Robert, 218
Newhart, Timothy, 218
Newhart, Virginia, 215-218, 220
Newman, Paul, 206
New York Times, The, 82, 155
Nightmare in Blood (film), v, 41, 73
Nichols, Mike, 2
Nimoy, Leonard, 222
Nine to Five (TV), 103
Nixon, President Richard, 211-212
Nodella, Burt, 112
Nolan, Bob, 176
Norris, Chuck, 222
North By Northwest (film), 114
Nothing in Common (film), 63
Nurse Diesel (character), 202

—O—

O'Connor, Carroll, 100
Odd Couple, The (play), 148
Offenbach, Jacques, 57
O'Flaherty, Terrence, 60
Old King Cole (character), 179
Omnibus (TV), 107
One Froggy Evening (cartoon), 55

O'Neill, Eugene, 61
Only When I Laugh (film), 80, 84
Ordinary People (film), 139
Orlando, Tony, 133
Orpheum Theater (San Francisco), 11, 15
Orwell, George, 53
Our Miss Brooks (radio-TV), 160, 164
Over the Santa Fe Trail (film), 174
Owl Gallery, 55

—P—

Pacific, The (TV), 67
Pacific Southwest Airlines, 37, 42
Paoli, Deno, 117
Paone, Marion, 77
Palace of Mystery (theater), 157
Pat Paulsen's Half-Hour Comedy Hour (TV), 128
Paulsen, Pat, 123-129, 196
Peckinpah, Sam, 101
Peewee Quartet, The
Pepe Le Pew (character), 49-50, 54
Pepsodent Show Starring Bob Hope, The (radio), 186
Pete 'n Tillie (TV), 75
Peter Gunn (TV), 150
Peterson, Axel, v
Peterson, Cassandra (see Elvira)
Phantom Planet, The (film), 47
Phantom Tollbooth, The (film), 55
Philadelphia (film), 63-64
Philco Playhouse (TV), 206
Phipps, Lloyd C., 166
Phyllis (TV), 207
Phyllis Diller Show, The (TV), 172
Pink Panther, The (film),
Platt, Ed, 1, 108, 114-117
Playboy (magazine), 136
Playhouse 90 (TV), 206
Pleshette, Suzanne, 220
Porky Pig (character), 50
Powell, William, 121

Prancer (film), 208
Price, Vincent, 222
Private Eyes, The (film), 153
Private's Affair, A (film), 191
Prize Fighter, The (film), 153
Producers, The (film), 108, 182
Promenade Theater, The (off-Broadway), 212
Pruitts of Southampton, The (TV), 169, 171-173
Psycho (book), 222
Purple Onion, The (club), 17, 21-24, 30-31, 35, 123, 128, 132-133, 135, 166-167, 171
Putch, William, 106-107
Pyle, Gomer (character), 21

—Q—

Quark (TV), 108
Quartet (film), 75
Queen Elizabeth, 216
Quiet Man, The (film), 174
Quinn, William, 215

—R—

Rack, The (film), 206
Randall, Tony, 192
Rawhide (TV), 222
Ray Bradbury Theater, The (TV), 80
Rebecca (film), 53
Rebel Without a Cause (film), 114
Red Knight Restaurant, 22
Reed, Rex, 82
Regalbuto, Joe, 152
Reiner, Rob, 100
Republic Studios, 136
Reynolds, Burt, 26
Rhythm Roundup (film), 174
Rich, David Lowell, 69, 73, 75
Richard Diamond (character), 149
Rickles, Don, 7, 33, 42, 96, 196, 217, 220
Ring of the Nibelungen (opera), 55
Rio Grande (film), 174, 176
Ripcord (TV), 176
Rivers, Joan, x

Road Pictures, ix, 186
Road Runner, The (cartoon), 49-50, 53-54
Road to Hong Kong, The (film), 186
Road to Rio, The (film), 186
Road to Singapore, The (film), 186
Roberts, Warren, 90
Rodd, Marsha, 87-88
Roddenberry, Gene, 222
Rodeberg, Janet, 30, 38, 42
Rogers, Roy, 136, 174
Romero, George A., 92
Roots (TV), 158
Rouvaun, 35
Rowan & Martin's Laugh-In (TV), 196
Rozsa, Miklos, viii
Rubin, Aaron, 21
Run a Crooked Mile (film), 139
Russell, Jane, 9, 222
Russell, Rosalind,

—S—

Sacramento State (college), 61
Sad Sack, The (character), 20
Sahl, Mort, 2, 7, 30, 196, 218
Sanders, George, 53
Sands Hotel (Las Vegas), 120, 217
San Francisco Chronicle, The, viii, 11, 32, 42, 60, 121, 130, 155, 163, 169
San Francisco Conservatory of Music, 191
San Francisco Giants, The, 37
San Francisco State (University), 28
San Jose Center for the Performing Arts, 130
San Jose Light Opera, 90
Santayana, George, 53
Santee (film), 117
Saving Mrs. Banks (film), 67
Saving Private Ryan (film), 66
Schell, Gregory James, 36
Schell, Ronnie, 1, 28-43
Schlesinger, Leon, 54
Schulman, Max, 216

Schultz, Al, 141-143
Schultz, Courtney, 143
Schultz, Garrett, 143
Schwarzenegger, Arnold, 222
Scolari, Peter, 60
Scott, George C., 112
Scubby Doo (TV), 38
Searchers, The (film), 174, 176
Second City (comedy team), 196
Second Greatest Entertainer in the Whole Wide World (play), 210-212
"Second Rhapsody" (tune),
Sellers, Peter, 181
Selznick, David O., 149
Serial, The (film), 132
Shaggy D.A., The (film), 149
Shakey's Pizza, 37
Shatner, Willilam, 222
Shawn, Dick, 209-213
Sheldon, Sidney, 192
Shelter Island, 94, 97
Sherlock Holmes (character), 153
Sherwood, Don, 29, 32, 38, 40
Shields and Yarnell, 132
Shot in the Dark, A (film), 80
Silent Movie (film), 183
Sills, Beverly, 75
Silver Bears (film), 132
Silver Streak (film), 48
Simon, John, 82
Simon, Mel, 69
Simon, Neil, 80
Simpson, Homer (character), 84
Sinatra, Frank, viii, 199
Six, Robert,
Skelton, Red, 218
Skuse, Dick, 119, 121-122
Sleepless in Seattle (film), 63, 65-66
Sleet. A; (character), 194, 197
Sly Fox (play), ix
Smith, Red, 119

Smothers Brothers, The, 101, 123, 125-128, 130-135, 216
Smothers Brothers Comedy Hour, The (TV), 123, 126, 129-130
Smothers Brothers Show, The (TV) 123
Smothers, Dick, 123, 130-135
Smothers, Tom, 123, 130-135
Smurfs, The (TV), 38
Sohl, Mort,
Some Like It Hot (film), 60
Somewhere in the Night (film),
Sondheim, Stephen,
Songs I Sing on the Jackie Gleason Show (album), 198
Sons of the Pioneers, 174, 176
South Shore Room, 8, 33
Spaceballs (film), 184
Spade, Sam (character), 149, 152
Spielberg, Steven, 46, 66
Spy Who Loved Me, The (film), 44-48
Stalling, Carl, 55, 57
Stanley, Erica, 18, 20, 29, 43, 65, 104, 144, 146, 203
Stanley, Russ, iv, 45, 67, 182
Stanley, Trista, iv, 85
Stanwyck, Barbara, 222
Stapleton, Jean, 100, 104-107
Stay Tuned (film), 57
Steiner, Max, viii
Steinhoff, Bud, 30
Stern, Howard, 121
Steve Allen Show, The (TV), 153
Stevens, Craig, 150, 152
Stewart, James, 222
Stewart, Michael, 15
St. Francis Hotel, 55
St. James Theater (Broadway), 12
Stone, Milburn, 177
Streets of San Francisco, The (TV), 222
Streisand, Barbra, 30
Stroker Ace (film), 26
Structure House (N.C.), 79
Struthers, Sally, 98-103, 107
Studio One (TV), 107, 206
Suds (TV), 39
Sullivan, Ed, 196
Sunday Datebook, viii, 155
Sutton, Frank, 20, 22-23, 31
Swamp Thing (film), 91
Sweeney, Bob, 160
Swiss Cheese (film), 80

—T—

TaleSpin (TV), 103
Taming of the Shrew, The (play), 62
Taslin, Frank, 54
Taylor, Rip, 38
Tenth Month, The (TV), 71
There Are Worst Things I Can Do (book), 93
There Goes the Bride (film), 132
There's a Girl in My Soup (film), 181
They Went That-a-Way & That-a-Way (film), 153
Thoroughly Modern Millie (film), 11, 139
Three for Two (TV),
Three Stooges, The, 1
Throw a Saddle on a Star (film), 174
Thursday's Game (TV), 219
Tim Conway Show, The (TV), 148, 154
Time magazine, 52, 158
Time of the Cuckoo, The (play), 106
Tinker, Grant, 139
Together Again (DVD), 154
Tom and Jerry (cartoon series), 55
Tommy Dorsey's Orchestra, 174
Tonight Show, The (TV), 217
Totem Pole Playhouse, The, 106
Toulouse-Lautrec, Henri, 50
Traynor, Carol (character), 90-91
T. R. Baskin (film), 182
"Treehouse of Horror IV" (TV episode), 84
"Tumbling Tumbleweeds" (song), 174
Turn-On (TV pilot), 154

Twelve Chairs, The (film), 179-183
Twiggy, 132
Twilight Zone, The (TV), 91
—U—
Ugliest Girl in Town, The (film), 60
Ultraman (TV), 38
Uncle Harry (character), 161
Up the Down Staircase (film), 107
Upton, Morgan, 73
—V—
Van Dyke, Dick, 32, 136, 138
Van Gogh, Vincent, 50
Van Patton, Joyce, 80
Verdoux-Feldon, Lucien, 111-112
Vinegar Free (TV), 106
Voyage to the Bottom of the Sea (film), 191
—W—
Wagner, Richard, 55
Wallerstein, Mike, 98
Wally's Café (play), 152
Walter, Jessica, 80
Warner, Jack L., 55, 205
Warner Bros. Symphony Orchestra, 55
Watchtower (magazine), 28
Wayne, John, 145, 174-175
Weaver, Dennis, 176
Webb, Jack, 152
Wedding, A (film), 75
What's Opera, Doc? (cartoon), 50, 55
White, Betty, 143
Who's Been Sleeping in My Bed? (film), 75
Who's Yehoodi? (cartoon), 186
Wilder, Billy, 60, 75
Wilder, Gene, 183-184, 220
Wilder, Thornton, 15
Wild, Wild West, The (TV), 47
Wile E. Coyote (character), 1, 49-50, 53-54, 56
Wilkins, Bob, 222
Williams, Guinn "Big Boy", 174
Williams, Robin, 7, 134

Willy the Plumber (character), 80
Wilson, Flip, 216
Winds of War (TV), 158
Wings of Eagles, The (film), 174
Windsor, Marie, 222
Winters, Jonathan, 7, 30-31, 183, 196, 216, 218
With Six You Get Eggroll (film), 196
Woodridge School, 163
Wooley, Sheb, 222
Would You Believe It? (book), 114
—Y—
Yang Pussy Cat, 110-112
Yarbro, Chelsea Quinn,
Yellow Rose, The (TV), 178
"You Can't Go Rolling Skating in a Buffalo Stampede" (song), 23
Young, Alan, 160
Young Frankenstein (film), 202
Youngman, Henny, 42
"Your Money or Your Life" (sketch)
—Z—
Zacherley, the Cool Ghoul aka John Zacherle (character), x, 156-157
Zimbalist, Efrem Jr., 206
Zolotov, Ivan (character), 212

OTHER BOOKS BY JOHN STANLEY

Available at His Website: www.stanleybooks.com
E-mail: creature@netwiz.net

THE GANG THAT SHOT UP HOLLYWOOD - Exclusive Interviews with Clint Eastwood on the set of *Magnum Force* (and four other encounters), Robert Mitchum, Chuck Norris, Paul Brinegar and Sheb Wooley of *Rawhide*, singer Frankie Laine, Karl Malden of *Streets of San Francisco*,
   James Stewart, Lauren Bacall, Jane Russell, Barbara Stanwyck, Marie Windsor . . . Exclusive History on the Marine Flag-Raisers on Iwo Jima. (Personally signed to the buyer)

I WAS A TV HORROR HOST - Exclusive Interviews with such sci-fi and horror icons as Ray Bradbury, Christopher Lee, Robert Bloch, Vincent Price, William Shatner, Leonard Nimoy, Gene Roddenberry, Elvira (Cassandra Peterson), Arnold Schwarzenegger, Bob Wilkins, Ray Harryhausen, William Castle, plus profiles of famous radio horror hosts. (Personally signed to the buyer)

LOST IN TIME AND SPACE WITH LEFTY FEEP - A lengthy exclusive interview with *Psycho* author Robert Bloch, with new photos taken by John Stanley, woven around nine Bloch short stories about Feep, a racetrack tout who is always falling into a world of fantasy. (Personally signed to the buyer)

THE CREATURE FEATURES MOVIE GUIDE STRIKES AGAIN. The fourth edition in what became a six-edition series. Featuring reviews of 5,614 genre movies of science-fiction, fantasy, and horror, with 232 photographs of popular monsters, actors, and historic scenes, 24 new sketches, and 1,709 cross references to secondary titles.

www.ingramcontent.com/pod-product-compliance
Lightning Source LLC
Chambersburg PA
CBHW062016220426
43662CB00010B/1353